Teach Yourself
VISUALLY™

Crocheting

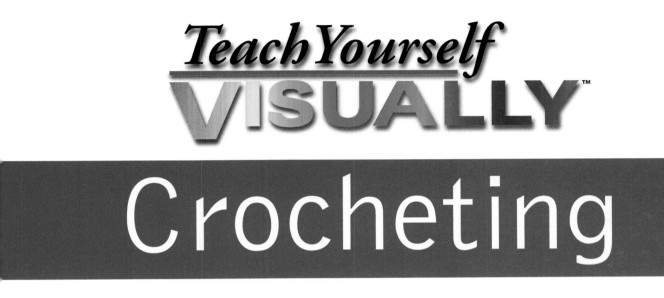

Crocheting

Visual

by Kim P. Werker and Cecily Keim

WILEY
Wiley Publishing, Inc.

Library of Congress Control Number: 2005923413

ISBN-13: 978-0-7645-9641-4
ISBN-10: 0-7645-9641-1

Printed in the United States of America

10 9 8 7 6 5 4 3 2 1

Book production by Wiley Publishing, Inc. Composition Services

Praise for the Teach Yourself VISUALLY Series

I just had to let you and your company know how great I think your books are. I just purchased my third Visual book (my first two are dog-eared now!) and, once again, your product has surpassed my expectations. The expertise, thought, and effort that go into each book are obvious, and I sincerely appreciate your efforts. Keep up the wonderful work!

—Tracey Moore (Memphis, TN)

I have several books from the Visual series and have always found them to be valuable resources.

—Stephen P. Miller (Ballston Spa, NY)

Thank you for the wonderful books you produce. It wasn't until I was an adult that I discovered how I learn—visually. Although a few publishers out there claim to present the material visually, nothing compares to Visual books. I love the simple layout. Everything is easy to follow. And I understand the material! You really know the way I think and learn. Thanks so much!

—Stacey Han (Avondale, AZ)

Like a lot of other people, I understand things best when I see them visually. Your books really make learning easy and life more fun.

—John T. Frey (Cadillac, MI)

I am an avid fan of your Visual books. If I need to learn anything, I just buy one of your books and learn the topic in no time. Wonders! I have even trained my friends to give me Visual books as gifts.

—Illona Bergstrom (Aventura, FL)

I write to extend my thanks and appreciation for your books. They are clear, easy to follow, and straight to the point. Keep up the good work! I bought several of your books and they are just right! No regrets! I will always buy your books because they are the best.

—Seward Kollie (Dakar, Senegal)

Credits

Acquisitions Editor
Pam Mourouzis

Project Editor
Suzanne Snyder

Copy Editor
Katie Robinson

Technical Editor
Jean Lampe

Editorial Manager
Christina Stambaugh

Publisher
Cindy Kitchel

Vice President and Executive Publisher
Kathy Nebenhaus

Interior Design
Kathie Rickard
Elizabeth Brooks

Cover Design
José Almaguer

Cover and Interior Photography
Matt Bowen

Special Thanks...

The following yarn companies generously supplied yarn for use in the tutorials and patterns in this book:

Blue Sky Alpacas
P.O. Box 387
St. Francis, MN 55070
www.blueskyalpacas.com

Crystal Palace Yarns
160 23rd St.
Richmond, CA 94804
www.straw.com

Elizabeth Austen, a Division of
Knitting Fever International
P.O. Box 336
315 Bayview Ave.
Amityville, New York 11701
www.knittingfever.com

Fleece Artist
1174 Mineville Rd.
Mineville, Nova Scotia
B2Z 1K8
Canada
www.fleeceartist.com

Hemp for Knitting
105 Park St.
Nelson, BC
V1L 2G5
Canada
www.hempforknitting.com

Lana Grossa Yarn (distributed
by Unicorn Books & Crafts)
1338 Ross St.
Petaluma, CA 94954
www.unicornbooks.com

Rio de la Plata Yarns
13603 Marina Pointe Dr.
Suite D-319
Marina Del Rey, CA 90292
www.riodelaplatayarns.com

Southwest Trading Company
1867 E. Third St.
Tempe, AZ 85281-2941
www.soysilk.com

About the Authors

Kim P. Werker is the founder and editor of Crochet me Online Magazine (www.crochetme.com), where she publishes hip and funky patterns and articles by recreational and professional crochet designers and enthusiasts. After a couple of earlier flings, Kim got addicted to crochet in her mid-20s. She is a professional member of the Crochet Guild of America and The National NeedleArts Association, and enjoys sharing her enthusiasm for the craft as a creative, stimulating, and relaxing medium of expression. Her next book will be published in the spring of 2006, and she's looking forward to more crochet-related endeavors in the future.

Originally from New York State, Kim now lives in Vancouver, BC, with her husband and their dog. When she sets down her hook and pen, she can be found skiing, reading, buying magazines, kicking back with friends, or knitting.

Cecily Keim documents her adventures in life, crocheting, and other creative endeavors at SuchSweetHands.com.

Throughout her life, regardless of the type of study or type of job, making things has always fascinated Cecily. Her great grandmother, Mama Mac, taught her to crochet at age 9. Cecily is mesmerized by the endless possibilities of crochet and loves passing on the enthusiasm as a writer, designer, and teacher.

Cecily lives in Los Angeles, watches too much television and loves candy, her cats, and her boyfriend. She teaches crochet classes at Unwind. You can also find her demonstrating her designs on the DIY channel's Knitty Gritty and Uncommon Threads.

Acknowledgments

This book has come about thanks to the contributions of many people to whom we are happily indebted. First and foremost we thank everyone at Wiley who has contributed to the various stages of the production of this book, especially Pam Mourouzis and Suzanne Snyder who provided patience, guidance, and a sincere interest in learning how to crochet. Matt Bowen's photographs could not be clearer or more beautiful, and we are so lucky that he was expertly able to show in pictures what we wrote in words. Kim also would like to thank her dad, Neil Piper, for taking her author photo.

We thank all of the companies that supplied us with yarn for the tutorials and patterns. We could not have shown off the wonders of crochet so effectively without them, and we appreciate the friendly and timely attention they paid us.

Cecily would love to thank Stephanie, Karyn, and everyone else at Unwind for support, feedback, and inspiration. She is honored also to be able to thank the wonderful family and friends that encourage her in all her crafty adventures.

Kim sends a shout-out to Cara at Birkeland Bros. Wool in Vancouver, BC, and to Angela for her ear and her support. She also sends big hugs to her parents, grandmother, and in-laws, who supported her and didn't think she was entirely nuts.

Thank you to Josi Hannon Madera, Vashti Braha, and Ana Voog for their photograph permissions, to Bruce Feller at Lantern Moon, and to the Craft Yarn Council of America for their permission to reprint information about industry standards.

We'd like to acknowledge the very active and supportive crochet community, at large. Your support and interest have given us this opportunity, and we look forward to serving you in the future.

Finally, thank you to Greg and to Rob, who loved us, encouraged us, and fed us yummy food throughout the months of tight deadlines, sleep deprivation, and marathon instant-message conversations. We love you both, and we can't wait for winter.

Table of Contents

Introduction to Crochet

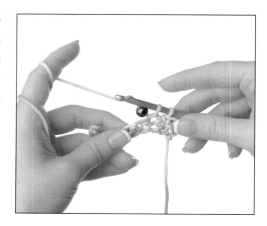

Tools and Yarn

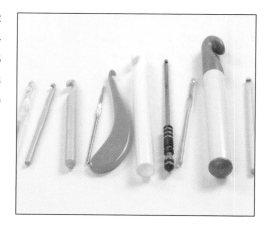

chapter **3** **Getting Started and Basic Stitches**

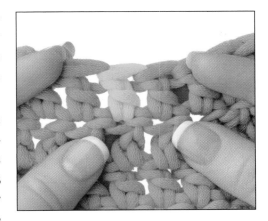

chapter 4 Basic Techniques

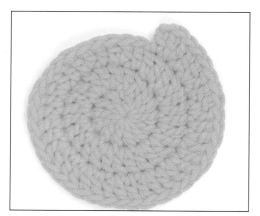

chapter 5 Stitch Variations

chapter 6 More Stitches

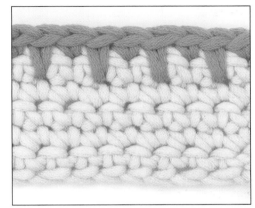

chapter 7 Combining Stitches

chapter 8 Follow a Pattern

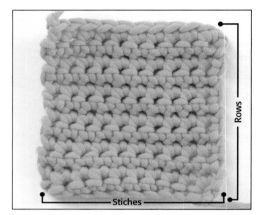

chapter 9 Stitch Patterns

chapter 10

Motifs and Fun Shapes

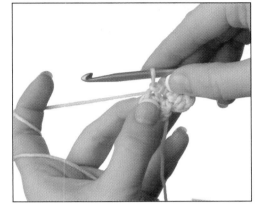

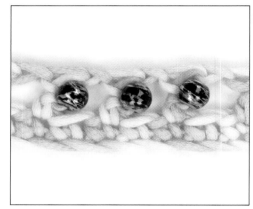

chapter 12 Final Details and Finishing

chapter 13 Simple Rectangles

chapter 1

Introduction to Crochet

Crochet is the process of interlocking loops of yarn with a hook. By combining a simple set of basic stitches, you can create an infinite assortment of items, be they accessories, garments, baskets, or home décor. We believe that crochet is both craft and art, and we hope you enjoy crocheting your own creations as much as we do!

Join the Crochet Community

This book gives you the information you need to learn crochet techniques, but you might also want to connect with crocheters in your community for help or to share your passion. This section will help you take advantage of resources in your community.

LOCAL YARN STORE

If you live in a large town or city, chances are you can find an independently owned and operated yarn store. Owners of yarn stores tend to be friendly, and many encourage crocheters to spend time in the store by having comfortable chairs and establishing a welcoming atmosphere. Yarn stores frequently offer crochet classes as well, so they can serve as a very helpful resource to you as you advance your crochet skills.

If you can't find a yarn store in your area, large craft stores tend to carry a selection of yarns, threads, and hooks and may offer crochet classes, too.

CROCHET GUILDS OR CLUBS

A crochet guild or club might already exist in your area. Such groups meet regularly for social crocheting and organize classes, fashion shows, charity events, and more. If you can't find a crochet guild or club in your area, you can contact the Crochet Guild of America (www.crochet.org) for information on how to start one.

INFORMAL CROCHET GROUPS

In many communities, informal groups meet regularly for social crocheting. Meeting at a member's home, at a coffee shop, or even at a bar, crochet clutches are a fun and easy way to connect with people who share your interest in crochet. Some yarn stores even organize social gatherings weekly or monthly. For more information, you can ask at your local store or do a search for groups in your area on www.crochet.meetup.com or groups.yahoo.com.

If you know how to knit, you may have encountered crochet in patterns that call for a crocheted edging or motif. Here are some tips that might help you pick up crochet without getting confused by what you already know about knitting.

The Differences

STITCHING

Crochet is worked with only one hook. Hold the hook in the hand you write with. Right- and left-handed crocheters produce the same fabric, just in opposite directions. Just because you use your hook with one hand does not mean your other hand is idle. Your *yarn hand* keeps your tension consistent, holds the body of your work, and helps guide your hook into tight places.

If you are a continental knitter (that is, you hold your yarn in your left hand and "pick" stitches with your right-hand needle), you may find it fairly easy to move into crocheting because you will continue to hold the yarn in your left hand and maneuver the hook with your right (if you are right-handed). If you are interested in learning how to knit in the continental style, you may find that knowing how to crochet helps you pick it up more smoothly. If you knit in the continental style, you may find that your experience holding yarn and keeping tension with your right hand translates easily to doing the same with your left.

In knitting, all stitches remain "open" or "active" throughout your project until you bind off at the end. In crochet, your stitches are bound off as you go; in most cases you have just one loop on your hook when you have completed a stitch.

GAUGE

In contrast to knitting stitches, crochet stitches are generally taller than they are wide. Therefore, you crochet more stitches over an inch than you do rows. It might take a bit of experience with crochet before your instincts adjust regarding how many stitches and rows you require to produce an item of certain dimensions.

Crochet stitches can feel denser than knitting stitches. You might find you are more comfortable using a hook that is larger than the needles you would use for the same yarn, to produce a fabric with good drape.

Crochet stitches use more yarn than knitting stitches, so when you purchase yarn for your first project, get more than you think you need. See Chapter 3 for more on estimating how much yarn to buy.

Find Resources on the Internet

The Internet offers an extensive, and rapidly expanding, amount of information about crochet. From patterns (free and for sale), yarns, and tools to message boards, magazines, and blogs, you can spend hours learning and connecting.

MESSAGE BOARDS

Also known as *forums,* message boards are websites that organize members' comments into threads related to specific topics of conversation. General crafts-related message boards, such as www.craftster.org, contain a section devoted to crochet. Also, crochet-only message boards, such as www.crochetville.org, devote themselves entirely to crochet. Other crochet-related websites have a message board encouraging discussions of topics related to that site specifically. (See www.crochetme.com/phpBB2/ as an example.)

Members of message boards ask questions of the other members in hopes of finding information about techniques or to request advice. Members also share photographs of their completed crochet projects, works in progress, and links to resources they find useful. Message boards are moderated by volunteers who ensure that conversations remain polite and on topic.

ONLINE MAGAZINES AND WEBSITES

Pioneered by enthusiastic crafters, websites devoted to making free craft patterns and related articles available to the public are becoming more and more abundant. *Crochet me Magazine* is an Internet-only publication that publishes original patterns, articles, and tutorials on its website every two months. Stitchguide.com reviews popular crochet stitches and provides illustrated and video tutorials. The Crochet Guild of America website offers tutorials, news, and patterns. See the list of crocheting organizations and their websites below.

BLOGS AND CROCHET ALONGS

A blog is an online diary or journal. The term *blog* comes from the term *web log.* Many software programs that simplify the blogging process are available free, which means that anyone with a computer and an Internet connection can have a blog. Blog software allows readers to leave comments in response to posts, so a community can develop around blogs centering around similar topics. Many crocheters maintain a blog devoted to their projects, displaying digital photographs of their completed projects and works in progress.

Belonging to an online community of like-minded crocheters allows for the sharing of tips, resources, advice, and often friendship. Crochet bloggers occasionally organize *crochet alongs*, during which each participant works on producing an item from the same pattern. This allows for a fun, shared experience, and more advanced crocheters can help beginners.

ONLINE STORES

Many local yarn stores have begun to sell yarn and tools through their websites, and more and more exclusively Internet-based yarn stores are starting up. If you find a pattern in which the yarn called for is unavailable in your area, you can easily find a store online that will ship the yarn to you. In addition, more and more crochet designers are choosing to sell their patterns online as Portable Document Format (PDF) files. This means that you are able to pay for a pattern and download it immediately, avoiding shipping costs.

Craftster.org
www.craftster.org

Crochet Guild of America
www.crochet.org

Crochet me Magazine
www.crochetme.com

Crochet Pattern Central
www.crochetpatterncentral.com

Crochetville Message Board
www.crochetville.org

Stitchguide.com
www.stitchguide.com

YarnStandards.com
www.yarnstandards.com

This book provides you with the skills and resources needed to enjoy a lifelong love of crochet. At some point, you may want to start crocheting without referring to a pattern. You might just want to try your hand at *designing* crochet items.

FIND INSPIRATION

Referring to books on crochet, textiles, sewing, weaving, and knitting provides inspiration and ideas for your own designs. Pay attention to the details around you: foliage, food, toys, architecture, clothing, music, books, and so on. Jot down your ideas so you don't forget.

The same methods used to approach free-form crochet can help you get into the process of designing a pattern. (See Chapter 9 for more on free-form crochet.)

GATHER YOUR TOOLS

When you have an idea for an item to crochet, you might just pick up your hook and make it, or you might plan the project out in advance. You'll need yarn, hooks of various sizes, a ruler or tape measure, a pencil and paper (sketch paper or graph paper), and a calculator.

TAKE CAREFUL NOTES

As you begin crocheting your design, take notes on your gauge, how many stitches you chain for your foundation, how many rows of each stitch you crochet, details of any combination stitches you use, where and how often you increase or decrease, and what the final dimensions of your piece are. These notes enable you to easily alter the pattern as you revise your design. You can then easily write a formal pattern from your notes.

This book contains many, many tutorials and tips. The following information can help you find what you're looking for. Although you might want to read the book from cover to cover, we have arranged the information so that you can easily skip around to learn about crochet in any order you'd like.

A Breakdown

CHAPTERS

This book is broken down into 14 chapters. We have organized the information into categories we find to be most useful. In Chapters 1 and 2, we introduce you to the craft of crochet, and hot to find resources to learn more about crochet and connect with other crocheters We also discuss the tools and materials you need to get started. Chapter 3 teaches you how to attach yarn to your hook to start a project and how to make the basic stitches that are the foundation of crochet.

Chapter 4 moves beyond simple stitching into shaping your work, crocheting in the round, and changing colors. Chapters 5 and 6 introduce several variations on the basic stitches.

Chapters 7 and 8 provide a basic stitch dictionary. These simple stitch patterns can be integrated into any project to add visual interest and texture.

Beginning in Chapter 8, we introduce how to follow a crochet pattern. In some sections we first present a "formal" pattern, complete with crochet shorthand and abbreviations, followed by a step-by-step explanation of the pattern in plain English. In other sections we simply present the "formal" pattern. We took care to write the patterns in a way that will be most accessible to novice crocheters. Keep in mind that each designer or publisher may have her own style of presenting patterns, so you may encounter subtle differences when you begin to follow patterns from other books, magazines, or web sites. Just remember that a pattern is simply a set of instructions that you should follow step-by-step.

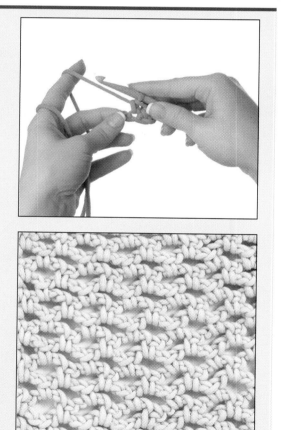

Chapter 9 tells you everything you need to know to understand and follow crochet patterns. We also provide some simple patterns to practice with while we introduce striping, textures, granny squares, and flowers.

Chapter 10 covers some special crochet techniques that sometimes involve very different stitches from the basics covered in Chapter 3. Chapter 11 walks you through fixing mistakes, finishing techniques, and basic embellishments.

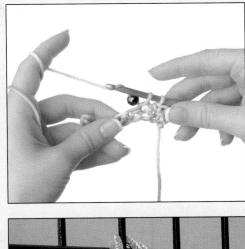

Chapter 12 provides several fun, basic patterns to get you started, and Chapter 13 contains more advanced patterns.

Chapter 14 concludes with useful information regarding preparing to crochet garments.

SECTIONS

Each chapter is broken down into sections according to the detailed topic being covered. You do not need to read sections in order. Just skip about the book as desired.

We understand that learning from a book can be difficult. We encourage you to seek out help in your community. Sometimes nothing compares to learning from another person, and you'll likely make many friends in the process.

We have very much enjoyed preparing the tutorials presented here. We wish you luck and hope you enjoy crochet as much as we do.

Enjoy!

2

Tools and Yarn

Before you start crocheting, take some time to familiarize yourself with the tools that will help you along the way. In this chapter, we introduce you to crochet hooks and notions, and you will learn all you need to know to choose the right yarns for your projects.

Crochet hooks come in many sizes and are made from a selection of different materials. The hook you choose to use depends in part on how big or small you want your stitches to be, and in part on your personal preference.

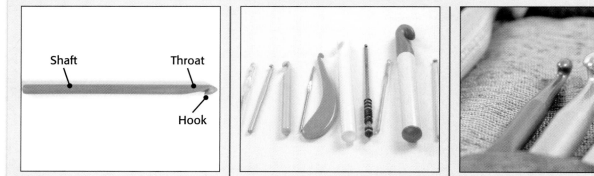

HOOK SHAPE

Crochet hooks are generally 5 to 7 inches in length. There is a hook at one end, which you use to grab yarn or thread and pull it through the stitches of your work. Various manufacturers shape their hooks differently, so try out a few different brands until you find the shape that you think works best. You hold the hook along its shaft, and there may be a flat section of the shaft to serve as a grip. Some hooks feature designs or embellishments at the end opposite the hook, but these are purely decorative and don't serve a function.

HOOK TYPES

Hooks are usually made from plastic, metal, wood, or bamboo. The smallest hooks are made of steel and are used with thin crochet thread to make intricately detailed items, such as doilies. Metal hooks can be very smooth, enabling the yarn to slide freely. Wood or bamboo hooks, on the other hand, provide a bit of friction with the yarn, which comes in handy when you're crocheting with slippery yarns. Experiment with different hooks until you find the ones that are the most comfortable to use. You might prefer to use certain types of hooks only with certain yarns.

HOOK SIZES

Hook size is determined by the diameter of the hook's shaft. Sizes range from tiny (0.75 millimeters/$^1/_{16}$ inch) to huge (20 millimeters/$^4/_5$ inch). Smaller hooks make small stitches; larger hooks make large stitches. Choose your hook size based on the recommended size for your yarn (see the section "Yarn Weight and Care Symbols" later in this chapter) and on how loose or tight you want your stitches to be.

Hook sizes are marked differently in the United States and the United Kingdom, although there is a growing move to standardize sizes by using metric measurements. Use the following tables to determine your hook size.

Hook Sizes		
Metric Size (in mm)	**U.S. Size**	**U.S. Knitting Needle Size**
2	A	0
2.25	B	1
2.75	C	2
3.25	D	3
3.5	E	4
3.75	F	5
4	G	6
4.5		7
5	H	8
5.5	I	9
6	J	10
6.5	K	10½
8	L	11
9	M/N	13
10	N/P	15
15	P/Q	19
16	Q	
19	S	35

Steel Hook Sizes	
Metric Size (in mm)	**U.S. Size**
0.75	#14
0.85	#13
1.0	#12
1.1	#11
1.3	#10
1.4	#9
1.5	#8
1.65	#7
1.8	#6
1.9	#5
2.0	#4
2.1	#3
2.25	#2
2.75	#1
3.25	#0
3.5	#00

In addition to hooks and yarn, you need other tools and notions to create neat, perfectly sized crocheted items. Keep these notions in a small case or kit so you always have them handy.

Use a *measuring tape* to take body measurements before you embark on crocheting a sweater or other fitted garment. A measuring tape also comes in handy when checking gauge. (See "Gauge" in Chapter 9.) You may also want a *stitch and row gauge,* designed to help you count how many stitches and rows you have created.

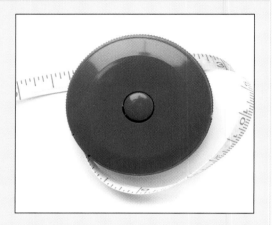

Occasionally you will come across a hook that's not marked for size because it is handmade or because the marking has worn off. Use a *hook gauge* to determine its size. Find the smallest hole that the shaft of the hook fits into; the size indicated beside that hole is the size of your hook. Hook gauges usually mark both metric and US sizes.

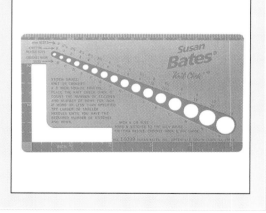

Stitch markers are useful in many situations. For example, when working in the round (see Chapter 4), you can mark the beginning of the round by placing a marker in the first stitch. You can buy stitch markers designed for this purpose or improvise with scraps of yarn or even earrings. When crocheting a garment, use stitch markers to indicate the placement of increases and decreases for shaping (see Chapter 4).

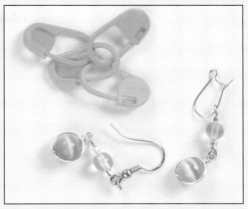
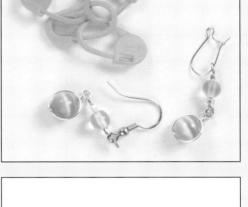

A *tapestry needle*, also called a yarn needle, has a blunt tip and a large eye to accommodate thick yarns. Use your needle to sew pieces together or to weave in yarn ends when you have completed your project. (See "Basic Finishing Techniques" in Chapter 4.)

Yarn Construction and Packaging

Buying yarn is one of the most exciting parts of starting a new crochet project. From color and texture to thickness and durability, your choice of yarn is as important as the pattern you follow. It is easier to choose yarn when you know a little about how it is constructed.

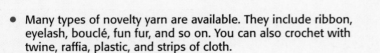

YARN CONSTRUCTION

Yarn construction can loosely be divided into two categories: traditional and novelty.

- Traditional yarn is spun by hand or by machine and is often *plied*. Plying consists of taking two or more strands of yarn and twisting them together to create a thicker, stronger yarn. These "smooth" yarns show stitches clearly.

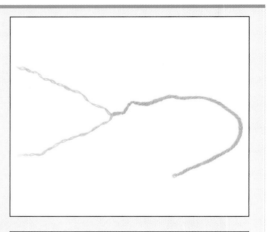

- Many types of novelty yarn are available. They include ribbon, eyelash, bouclé, fun fur, and so on. You can also crochet with twine, raffia, plastic, and strips of cloth.

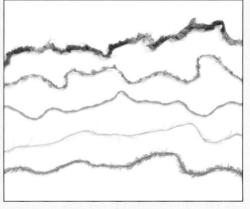

YARN PACKAGING

Store-bought yarn is packaged in one of two ways.

Hank: The yarn is wound into a circle twisted onto itself, creating an attractive, compact skein (a). Yarn pulled from a hank tangles easily and is difficult to undo. Instead wind before use. (See "Winding.")

Center-pull skein: The yarn is wound into a cylinder. Unwind from the outside or pull the end out from the inside (b). This results in fewer tangles and prevents the skein from rolling around as you draw yarn from it.

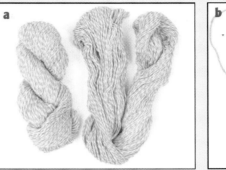

WINDING

Before you start crocheting with yarn that was packaged in a hank, you have to wind the yarn into a ball or a center-pull skein. (See the preceding section, "Yarn Packaging.") You can wind the yarn into a ball by hand or use a *yarn winder* to produce a center-pull skein (which is sometimes called a *cake* due to its shape).

TIP

Some yarns tangle easily regardless of how well wound they are. To help avoid this problem, keep your wound yarn in a plastic sandwich bag, with the yarn fed through a small opening at the top.

Some yarns, especially some wools, are very delicate and can break easily. Avoid tugging on yarn to prevent breakage.

Yarn Fibers

In addition to choosing the type of yarn construction you'd like to work with, you have to choose a fiber or fiber blend. The type of material a yarn is spun or manufactured from has a great effect on your final product. Consider whether your project should be warm, be durable, be machine washable, breathe well—the list goes on!

Different Types

NATURAL FIBERS

Natural fibers come from plants or animals. Perhaps the most common natural fibers are cotton and wool, but there are many others.

Plant fibers are usually lightweight, are machine washable, have little stretch, and breathe well. They include cotton, linen, soy, hemp (as shown here), bamboo, and jute.

Animal fibers are very warm (even when wet), have a bit of natural stretch, breathe well, and generally must be washed by hand. They include wool, mohair (shown here), cashmere, silk, angora, and alpaca.

SYNTHETIC FIBERS

Synthetic fibers are manmade. They include acrylic, nylon, rayon, and polyester. Some synthetics are less expensive than natural fibers, and they tend not to breathe as well. However, as technology advances, synthetic fibers have an increasing number of desirable qualities, including durability, softness, and vibrancy of color.

NOVELTY YARNS

Frequently made from synthetic materials, novelty yarns come in a wide variety of textures and shapes. These include eyelash, faux fur, bouclé, ladder, beaded—the list goes on. Novelty yarns can be used alone or combined with other yarns to create very unique crocheted items. It may not be practical to create entire garments or home décor items solely out of novelty yarns, but they are particularly suited to trims, accents, and accessories.

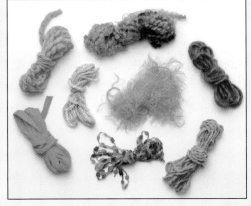

TERMS

You will encounter the following terms when choosing yarns:

- *Superwash:* This term applies to yarns made from wool, wool blends, and other animal fibers that have been chemically treated to prevent them from *fulling* (shrinking and becoming very dense) when they are agitated in a washing machine or by hand.

- *Mercerized:* This term applies to cotton that has undergone a specific chemical treatment resulting in yarn that is strong, is high in luster, and takes dye extremely well.

All the information you need to know about yarn is contained on its label. This section covers how to determine the amount of yarn contained in a skein and introduces the importance of the dye lot.

LENGTH

When it comes time to figure out how many skeins of yarn you're going to need for a particular project, you need to know how many yards each skein contains (for example, 100 yards/4 ounces or 75 meters/50 grams). It is important to buy yarn according to length and not weight. A 4-ounce skein of lace-weight yarn might contain 1,200 yards, while 4 ounces of bulky-weight yarn might contain just 45 yards.

DYE LOT

Yarns are dyed in limited quantities, called *dye lots*. This may result in minor variations between lots of the same color. Yarn manufacturers stamp each label with the code for the dye lot of the yarn. To avoid color inconsistencies when you require multiple skeins of the same colored yarn, make sure that you purchase all skeins from the same dye lot.

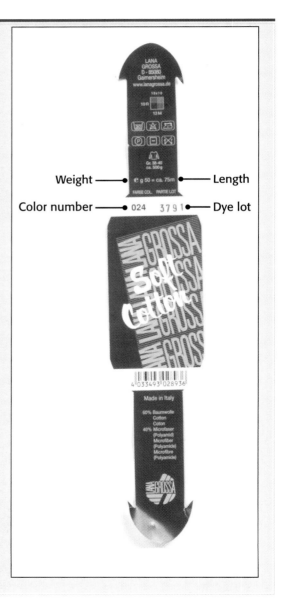

If you don't already have a growing collection of yarn intended for crochet projects, you will soon. To prevent future frustration, it's important to store and care for your yarn stash.

KEEP YARN CLEAN AND DRY

Unused yarn should be stored in a clean, dry place to protect it from pests and dirt. Although keeping yarn in an airtight bag is a good idea for a limited time, it is important to let natural fibers breathe. Keep wools safe from moths by storing them with cedar chips, lavender sachets, or mothballs.

KEEP YARN ORGANIZED

As your yarn collection grows, you will thank yourself for keeping it organized. You may want to organize your yarn by project, by fiber, by weight, or by color. It doesn't matter how you organize it as long as you can easily find the yarn you want! Keep all balls from the same dye lot together so that you know how much you have to work with when a potential project comes up.

The number of storage devices you can use to house your yarn is infinite, but here are a few suggestions:

- Baskets are attractive and can be used as decoration in your home.
- Clear, plastic drawers keep your yarn clean and easy to find.
- A bookshelf looks lovely filled with neatly stacked skeins of yarn.

Yarn Weight and Care Symbols

Yarn comes in a multitude of weights. From the thinnest lace weight to the thickest super bulky yarns, it is important for you to choose hooks and patterns that are appropriate for the weight of yarn you use. Once your project is completed, keep the yarn label so you know how to care for it properly.

RECOMMENDED HOOK SIZE

Most yarn labels show a recommended hook size to use with the yarn. In some instances, the label provides only a recommendation for knitting needle size. In this case, use a hook of the same or slightly larger metric size. (If you are using US sizing, find the US size equivalent to the metric size given for the recommended knitting needles.)

Note: *See section "Hooks" for more information on equivalent hook sizes.*

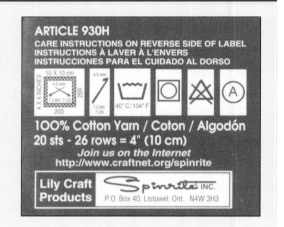

YARN WEIGHT SYMBOLS

Be it the thinnest crochet thread (10 stitches per inch) or the bulkiest yarn (2 stitches per inch), it's important to figure how the weight of yarn you choose will affect your choice of pattern and hook. The Craft Yarn Council of America has created the following recommendations regarding yarn weight, which can help you use the information found on yarn labels.

Yarn Weight Category Names	Type of Yarns in Category	Crochet Gauge* Ranges in Single Crochet to 4 inch	Recommended Hook in Metric Size Range	Recommended Hook in U.S. Size Range
SUPER FINE	Sock, Fingering, Baby	21–32 sts	2.25–3.5 mm	B–1 to E–4
FINE	Sport, Baby	16–20 sts	3.5–4.5 mm	E–4 to 7
LIGHT	DK, Light Worsted	12–17 sts	4.5–5.5 mm	7 to I–9
MEDIUM	Worsted, Afghan, Aran	11–14 sts	5.5–6.5 mm	I–9 to K–10½
BULKY	Chunky, Craft, Rug	8–11 sts	6.5–9 mm	K–10½ to M–13
SUPER BULKY	Bulky, Roving	5–9 sts	9 mm and larger	M–13 and larger

* GUIDELINES ONLY: The above reflect the most commonly used gauges and needle or hook sizes for specific yarn categories.

CARE SYMBOLS

Although some yarn labels spell out how to wash and dry items made from that particular yarn, universal yarn care symbols are also frequently used. To avoid accidentally ruining the gorgeous crocheted item you have spent hours creating, refer to the following chart to interpret yarn care symbols.

Getting Started and Basic Stitches

In this chapter, learn how to begin a crochet project and how to form basic stitches. From attaching yarn to your hook to working in rows, all the basics are covered.

There are different ways to hold a crochet hook. It is important that you find a grip that is comfortable and allows you to relax while you crochet.

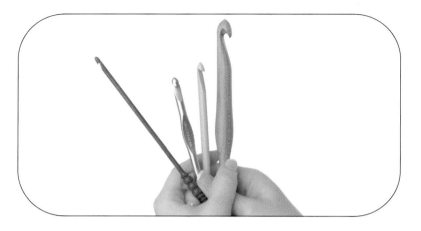

The Hook Hand

Hold your hook in the hand you write with. This hand is in charge of controlling the hook and maneuvering it into and out of the stitches as you work.

You can hold the hook like a pencil...

...or like a knife.

Do what comes naturally as long as you can comfortably control the hook. Hold the hook firmly but not too tightly.

Since you control your hook with one hand, you use your other hand to hold your yarn so that it flows freely but maintains an even tension. Although it seems like your hook hand does all the work, your yarn hand performs an essential role!

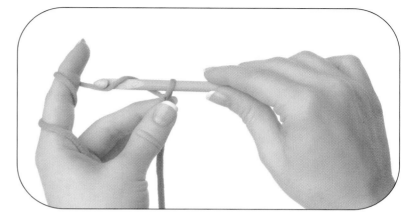

The Yarn Hand

The yarn hand is just as important as the hook hand. In fact, the yarn hand does double duty, holding the body of your work and controlling the yarn.

The yarn is attached to the hook with a slip knot. (See the section "Make a Slip Knot.")

Your middle finger and thumb hold the tail of yarn that dangles from the hook and hold the fabric you are creating.

Use your index finger to hold and guide the yarn. Gently wrap the yarn once or twice around your index finger to achieve the control you need. The yarn should be taut but should slide easily along the hook as you make stitches.

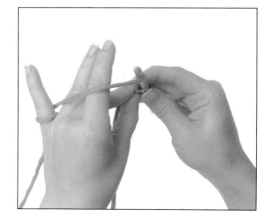

Another popular way to control the yarn is to wrap the yarn around your pinky finger, then behind your other fingers, and finally over your index finger.

TIP

Everyone holds and guides her yarn differently. The guidelines above provide a good place to start. Work from here to see what's best for you! When both hands are relaxed, the stitches move easily on the hook.

Choose a Learning Yarn and Hook

Starting with a smooth, simple, light-colored yarn will help you concentrate on the stitches and on the process of crocheting. You will soon become familiar with your stitches, and using textured novelty yarns will be easier.

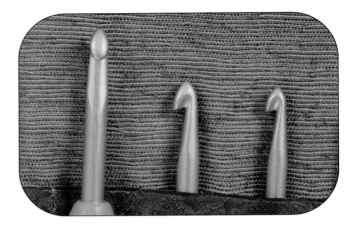

Choose a Yarn

Use the simplest yarn you can find. It should be smooth and durable. If the yarn frays, unravels, or untwists easily, it won't stand up well to the learning process, during which you will frequently need to pull out mistakes.

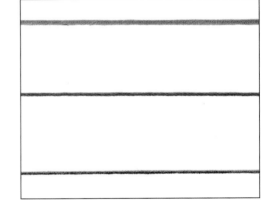

Choose a yarn that allows you to see your stitches clearly. Avoid fuzzy, heavily textured yarns. Dark colors make it hard to see the stitches as you are learning, so pick a light color.

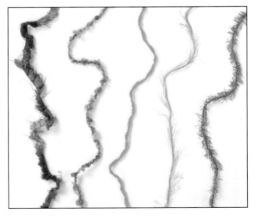

Choose a Hook

Start with the hook size recommended on the yarn label. If you find that your stitches are too tight, switch to a larger hook. If your stitches are too loose, switch to a smaller hook. You should be able to easily insert your hook into the stitches you make, and you should feel comfortable with the shape of the hook shaft and the hook itself.

Note: See Chapter 2 for more on hooks and on reading labels.

Suggested Learning Yarns and Corresponding Hook Sizes		
Company	**Yarn Name**	**Hook Size**
Lana Grossa	Soft Cotton	6.0 mm–8.0 mm
Lana Grossa	New Cotton	4.0 mm–5.0 mm
Blue Sky Alpacas	Organic Cotton	4.5 mm–5.5mm
Southwest Trading Company	Optimum	4.5 mm–5.5mm
Patons	Grace	3.5 mm–4.5 mm
Lion Brand	Wool Ease	4.5 mm–5.5 mm
Red Heart	SuperSaver	5.5 mm
Caron	Simply Soft	5.0 mm
Cascade	220	4.5 mm–5.5 mm

Notes for Left-Handed Crocheters

Most books and patterns are written from a right-handed perspective. Here is some information for lefties that will come in handy as you progress through this book.

Crochet Left-Handed

Here are some important techniques, illustrated for lefties.

This is the suggested way to hold the yarn and the hook. (See the sections "How to Hold Your Hook" and "How to Hold Your Yarn" for suggestions for righties.)

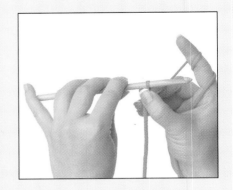

This is a yarn over as performed by a leftie. (See the section "Make a Chain Stitch" for more information on yarn overs.) Lefties work crochet stitches from left to right across their rows instead of from right to left.

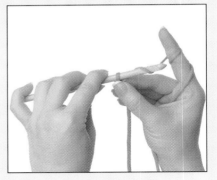

TIP

Lefties Learning from Righties

When learning from a right-handed crocheter, sit facing each other instead of side by side. This allows you to mirror right-handed actions.

Mirror images of right-handed graphics may also help ease confusion. Hold a small mirror to the side of an image or use a photocopier to create mirror images.

Don't worry if your left-handed stitches look different from the pictures you see. Left-handed stitches slant differently, but that isn't wrong!

A slip knot is used to attach the yarn to the hook. Making the knot is the first step in beginning any project.

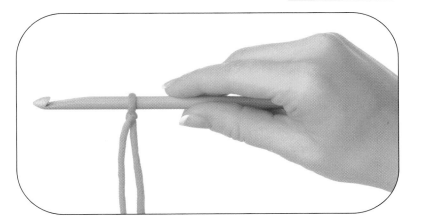

Slip Knot

① Create a loop with your yarn, leaving at least a 6-inch tail (a).

② Place the loop on top of the tail (b).

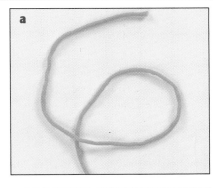
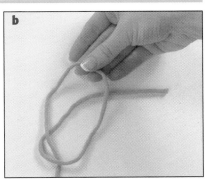

③ Insert the hook into the loop and under the tail (a).

④ Hold both ends of the yarn and pull gently to tighten (b).

The slip knot should be tight enough on the hook that there is no space between the yarn and the hook, but loose enough that the knot slides easily.

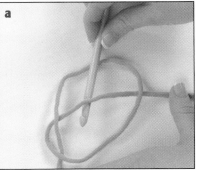
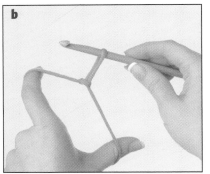

The chain stitch is used to create a foundation for most crochet work as well as to create space between other stitches in openwork or lace patterns. Its pattern abbreviation is CH or ch.

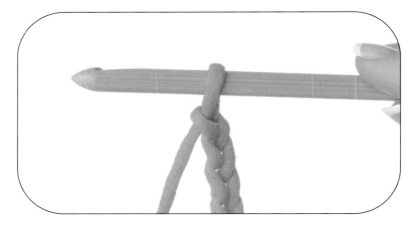

Make a Chain Stitch

1 Start with a slip knot on the hook.

Note: *See the section "Make a Slip Knot" for more information.*

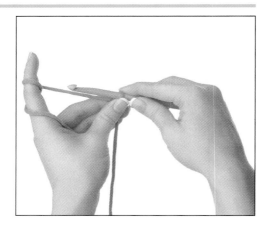

2 Yarn over.

To do a yarn over, wrap the yarn over your hook from back to front so that the yarn is coming toward you.

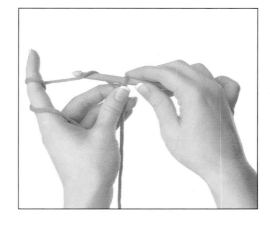

3 Draw the yarn through the first loop on your hook (the slip knot).

You've made 1 chain stitch. There is also 1 loop left on the hook.

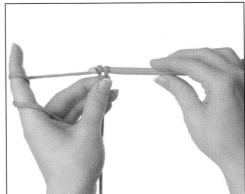

4 Yarn over. Draw the yarn through the loop created by the last chain stitch made.

5 Repeat step 4 until you have made the desired number of chain stitches. (Do not count the slip knot as a chain. Also, do not count the loop on the hook.) Adjust your hold on the chain as it grows so that you're always holding it near the hook.

Keep the chain hanging down from the hook. Do not let the stitches you've made twist around on the hook.

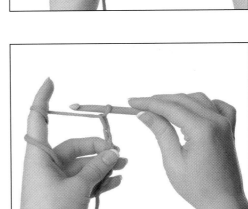

TIP

After each stitch, *do not* tighten the chain you've just made. Resist the urge to control your stitches by pulling them tight. If your chain is too tight, it will be very difficult to work stitches into it later. You should have enough room to poke your hook through each chain stitch.

Too tight

Perfect

Make a Foundation Chain

To begin a crochet project, you must start with a chain into which you will work your first row of stitches. Use the chain stitch to create this foundation.

Chain 12. Now take a close look at your chain.

The side facing you as you work the chain stitches looks like a braid.

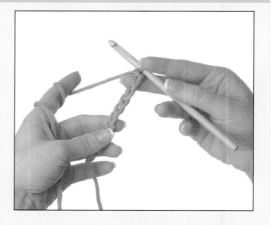

The back of the chain has a ridge down the middle, almost like a spine. There should be 12 chain stitches. Never count the loop on the hook or the slip knot.

For most patterns and swatches, you work a chain for every stitch you plan to have in the first row, plus additional chains to serve as your first turning chain.

Note: *See the section "Make a Turning Chain" for more information.*

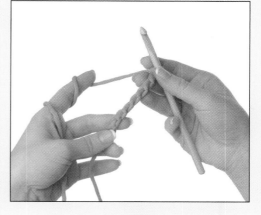

Work your stitches into whichever part of the chain you are most comfortable with. The examples in this book work into one loop of the chain.

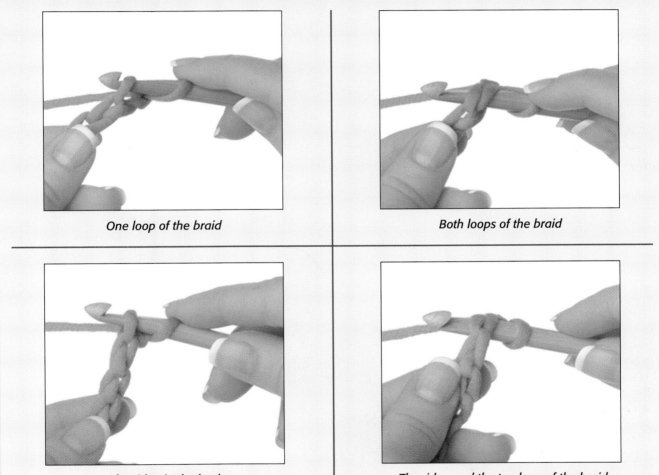

One loop of the braid

Both loops of the braid

The ridge in the back

The ridge and the top loop of the braid

Crochet stitches can be quite tall. You use chain stitches at the beginning or end of a row to create the height required by the stitches you are making. These turning chains (so called because you make them before or after turning your work at the end of a row) also keep the edges of your work neat and even.

The total stitches required for the turning chain are added to the number needed in the foundation chain for the stitch pattern.

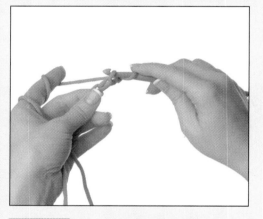

For example, for a row of 5 single crochet stitches, the foundation chain is 6 chains.

For a row of 5 double crochet stitches, the foundation row is 8 chains.

Each Stitch Requires a Specific Number of Turning Chains at the Beginning or End of a Row	
Stitch	**Number of Turning Chains**
Slip stitch	0
Single crochet	1
Half double crochet	2
Double crochet	3
Treble crochet	4

Note: See the sections on specific stitches for more information on the number of turning chains required.

TIP

- This chart is only a guide. With experience, you may find that you prefer to use fewer chains to create a turning chain.
- Turning chains can be made at the end or beginning of a row. Crochet patterns may specify where to make the chains; if your pattern does not, follow your personal preference.

The slip stitch creates the tightest, shortest, and stiffest of the crochet stitches and is frequently used to stitch squares or panels together when assembling an afghan or other large piece. Its pattern abbreviation is *SL ST, sl st, Sl st,* or *SS.*

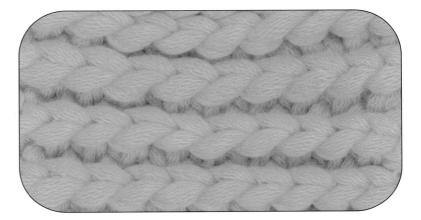

Slip Stitch

To begin a project with a row of slip stitch, create a foundation chain (see "Make a Foundation Chain") equal to the number of slip stitches you require. Work your first slip stitch into second chain from your hook.

① Insert hook into next stitch (a).

② Yarn over and draw yarn through stitch and through loop on hook (b).

One slip stitch created.

③ Repeat steps 1 and 2 until you have completed your first row of slip stitch.

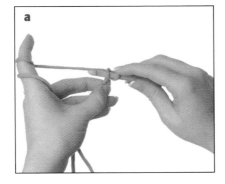
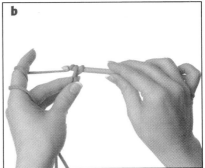

④ Turn the piece. Insert your hook through both loops at the top of the first stitch from the previous row. Follow steps 1 and 2.

Note: Slip stitches are very tight when worked in full rows. Take care to keep your tension loose, or use a hook that is larger than recommended.

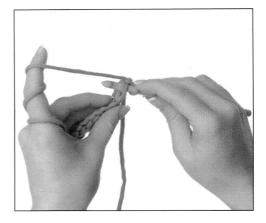

Make a Single Crochet

The single crochet stitch is the basic foundation of crochet. Most other stitches are variations on this stitch. Its pattern abbreviation is *sc* or *SC*.

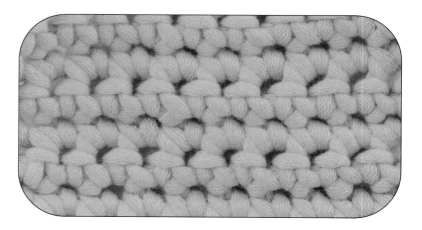

Single Crochet

To begin a project with a row of single crochet, create a foundation chain (see the section "Make a Foundation chain") equal to the number of single crochet stitches you require, plus 1. Work your first single crochet into the second chain from your hook. Continue to the end of the chain. Turn.

1 Insert your hook into the next stitch, then yarn over by wrapping the yarn around the hook from back to front.

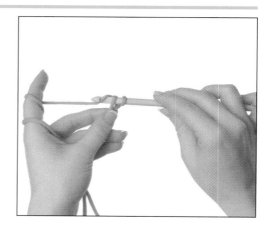

2 Draw the yarn through the stitch.

There are now 2 loops on the hook.

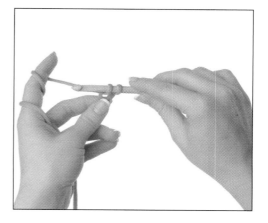

3 Yarn over and draw the yarn through both loops on the hook.

There is now 1 loop on the hook.

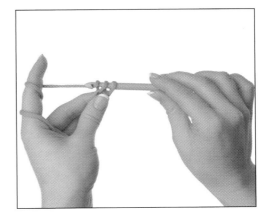

4 One single crochet created.

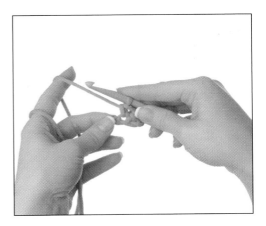

5 Repeat steps 1–4 until you have completed your first row of single crochet. Chain 1 to create a turning chain (a).

Note: For more on turning chains, see the section "Make a Turning Chain."

6 Turn the piece. Insert your hook through both loops at the top of the first stitch from the previous row (b). Follow steps 1–4.

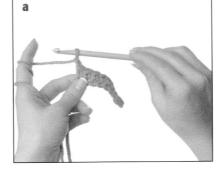

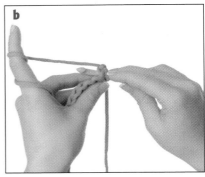

Make a Half Double Crochet

Half double crochet is a versatile stitch that is commonly used to make garments, hats, and other accessories. Its pattern abbreviation is *hdc* or *HDC*.

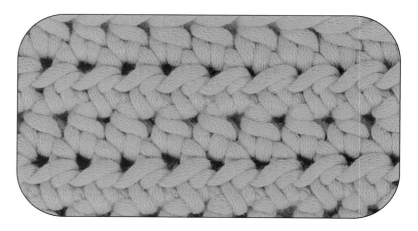

Half Double Crochet

To begin a project with a row of half double crochet, create a foundation chain (see the section "Make a Foundation Chain") equal to the number of half stitches you require, plus 2. Work your first half double crochet into the third chain from your hook. Continue to the end of the chain. Turn.

1 Yarn over once.

2 Insert your hook into the next stitch, yarn over, and draw the yarn through the stitch (a).

There are now 3 loops on the hook.

3 Yarn over and draw the yarn through all three loops on the hook (b).

One loop remains on the hook. One half double crochet created.

Continue to follow steps 1–3 until you have completed your first row of half double crochet. Chain 2 to create a turning chain.

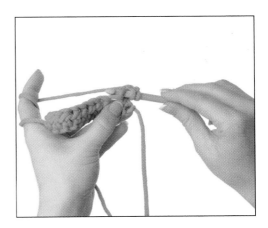

 Turn the piece. Skip the first stitch at the beginning of the row. The turning chain is counted as the first half double crochet of the row. Follow steps 1–3 to create a half double crochet in the second stitch of the row.

Note: *For more on turning chains, see the section "Make a Turning Chain."*

Remember to insert the hook through both of the loops at the top of the stitch from the previous row.

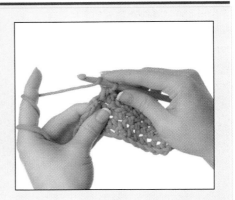

TIP

Because the turning chain counts as the first half double crochet at the beginning of a row, you work into it as though it is a half double crochet.

Make a Double Crochet

Like half double crochet, you make a double crochet stitch by doing a yarn over before inserting your hook into the next stitch. Its pattern abbreviation is *DC* or *dc*.

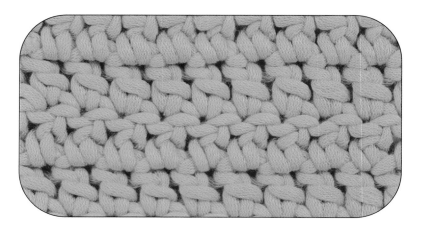

Double Crochet

To begin a project with a row of double crochet, create a foundation chain (see the section "Make a Foundation Chain") equal to the number of double crochet stitches you require, plus 3. Work your first double crochet into the fourth chain from your hook. Continue to the end of the chain. Turn.

1 Yarn over once.

2 Insert your hook into the next stitch, yarn over, and draw the yarn through the stitch (a).

There are now 3 loops on the hook.

3 Yarn over and draw the yarn through the first 2 loops on the hook (b).

There are now 2 loops on the hook.

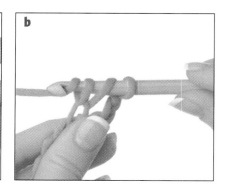

④ Yarn over and draw the yarn through the 2 remaining loops on the hook (a).

One double crochet created (b).

⑤ Continue to follow steps 1–4 until you have completed your first row of double crochet.

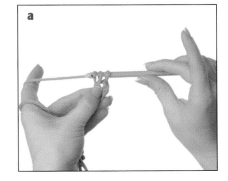

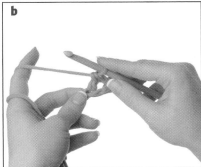

⑥ Chain 3 to create a turning chain (a). Turn the piece. Skip the first stitch at the beginning of the row. The turning chain counts as the first double crochet of the row. Follow steps 1–4 to create a double crochet in the second stitch of the row.

Note: *For more on turning chains, see the section "Make a Turning Chain."*

Remember to insert the hook through both of the loops at the top of the stitch from the previous row (b).

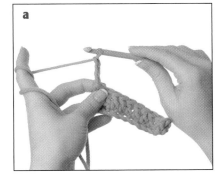

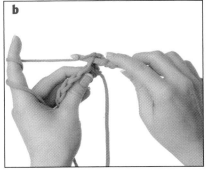

TIP

Because the turning chain counts as the first double crochet at the beginning of a row, you work into it as though it is a double crochet.

Treble crochet (also called triple crochet) is a very tall stitch, which you create by making two yarn overs before inserting your hook into the next stitch. The tall stitches create a fabric with more drape than the single crochet or half double crochet stitches. Its pattern abbreviation is *tr* or *TR*.

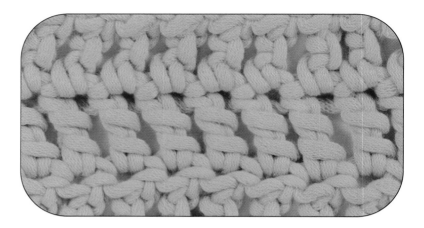

Treble Crochet

To begin a project with a row of treble crochet, create a foundation chain (see the section "Make a Foundation Chain") equal to the number of treble crochet stitches you require, plus 4. Work your first treble crochet into the fifth chain from your hook. Continue to the end of the chain. Turn.

1 Yarn over twice.

2 Insert your hook into the next stitch, yarn over, and draw the yarn through the stitch (a).

    There are now 4 loops on the hook (b).

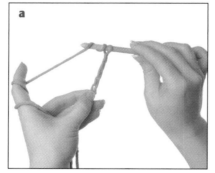

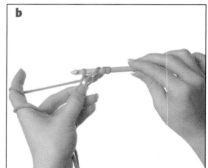

3 Yarn over and draw the yarn through the first 2 loops on the hook.

    There are now 3 loops on the hook (a).

4 Yarn over and draw the yarn through the next 2 loops on the hook.

    There are now 2 loops on the hook (b).

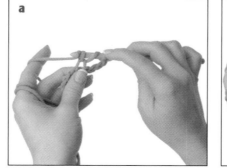

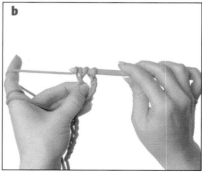

⑤ Yarn over and draw the yarn through both loops on the hook (a).

One treble crochet created (b).

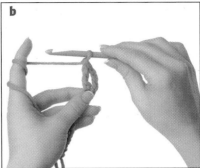
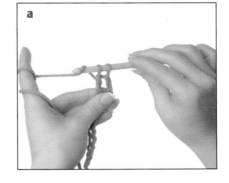

⑥ Continue to follow steps 1–5 until you have completed your first row of treble crochet. Chain 4 to create turning chain (a).

Note: For more on turning chains, see "Make a Turning Chain."

⑦ Turn the piece. Skip first stitch at beginning of row. The turning chain counts as first treble crochet of row. Follow steps 1–5 to create a treble crochet in second stitch of row.

Remember to insert hook through both loops at top of stitch from previous row (b).

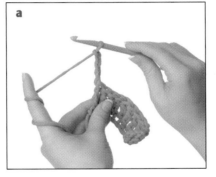
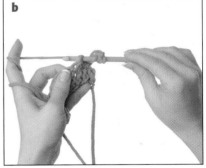

TIP

Because the turning chain counts as the first treble crochet at the beginning of a row, you work into it as though it is a treble crochet.

You need to count the number of stitches in each row or round of your work to determine whether you are achieving the correct gauge for the pattern you have chosen. It is also important to keep track of how many stitches are in a working piece—often, counting stitches is the best way to diagnose mistakes.

Count Your Stitches

There are two easy ways to identify an individual stitch in your work:

- The first way is to examine the tops of the stitches. The top of each crochet stitch looks like the chain stitch (or like a braid). Each chain corresponds to one stitch.

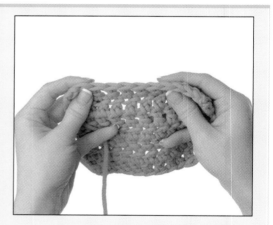

- The second way is to examine the *post* of the stitch. The post (a) is the "body" of the stitch, stemming down from the top chain, mentioned previously, to the top of the stitch from the previous row. Just count the posts to see how many stitches you have made (b).

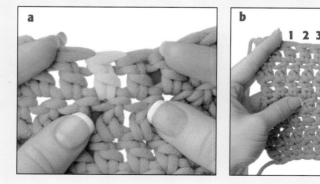

The hook size you use affects the size of the stitches you create; a large hook creates large stitches, while a small hook creates small stitches. The hook size you choose affects the fabric you create just as much as your choice of yarn, stitch, and pattern.

RECOMMENDED HOOK SIZE

Most yarn labels indicate the hook size recommended for that particular weight of yarn (see the section "Yarn Weight and Care Symbols" in Chapter 2), and patterns indicate the hook size used by the designer. Using a hook that is close to the recommended hook size results in a solid fabric that is neither too tight nor too loose, as you can see in the middle swatch. If you crochet tightly, you may need to use a hook that is one or two sizes larger than the recommended size to obtain the required gauge. If you crochet loosely, you may need to use a hook that is one or two sizes smaller to achieve the required gauge.

MUCH LARGER HOOK SIZE

Crocheting with a hook much larger than the recommended size for your yarn, like the bottom swatch, results in loose, open stitches that appear lacey and have excellent drape. Experiment with large hooks for making items such as scarves, shawls, and lacy cardigans.

Note: Drape refers to how well the fabric "flows." Fabrics with good drape are flexible and move freely when worn; fabrics with little drape feel stiff and boxy.

MUCH SMALLER HOOK SIZE

Crocheting with a hook much smaller than the recommended size for your yarn results in tight stitches and an overall stiff fabric, as you can see in the top swatch. Experiment with small hooks for making items such as baskets, bags, and bowls.

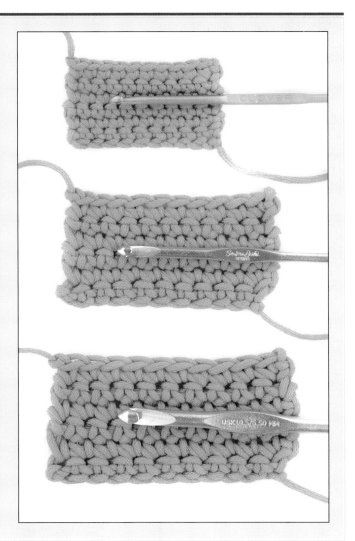

Whether you are following a pattern or designing your own crocheted garment, you need to start with the measurements of the person who will wear the piece when it is completed. Having correct measurements enables you to create a garment that fits properly and is flattering.

MEASURE YOUR BUST

Standing tall, wrap the tape measure around your bust or chest at the fullest part, taking care not to wrap the tape measure too tightly. Take note of the measurement and use it when deciding how much *ease* you would like your crocheted top to have. Ease describes how snugly or loosely a garment will fit.

If you always wear a bra under a sweater, be sure to take your measurements while wearing a bra so that your sweater will fit properly.

MEASURE YOUR WAIST

Standing tall, wrap the tape measure around the narrowest part of your waist, taking care not to wrap the tape measure too tightly. Take note of the measurement. Use this measurement to figure how many stitches to increase and/or decrease to shape your top at the midsection.

MEASURE YOUR HIPS

Wrap the tape measure around your hips, over the widest part of your behind. Take care not to wrap the tape measure too tightly. Take note of the measurement. Use this measurement to determine how wide the bottom sweater hem should be if it is going to be long enough to cover your hips.

MEASURE YOUR ARM LENGTH

Hold the tape measure from your armpit to your cuff, with your arm slightly bent. Use this measurement to determine sleeve length.

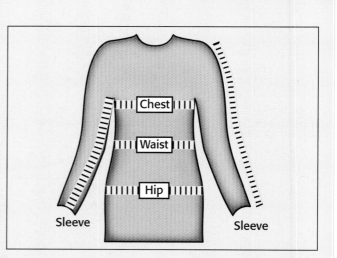

MEASURE THE WIDTH OF YOUR BACK

Hold the tape measure from the outside of one shoulder to the outside of the other shoulder, across your back. Use this measurement to determine how wide the back of your sweater should be.

MEASURE YOUR TORSO

Hold the tape measure beginning at the most prominent bone at the base of your neck, and extend it to your natural waistline. This measurement helps you determine where to place waist-shaping decreases and increases.

MEASURE YOUR HEAD

Wrap the tape measure across your forehead and around the circumference of your head, keeping the measuring tape snug. Use this measurement to determine what size to make a hat.

KEEP A MEASUREMENT NOTEBOOK

Make a note of your measurements in a notebook that you can keep handy. Also make note of the measurements of people for whom you frequently crochet garments. Having this information readily available helps you determine how much yarn to purchase for a given project and saves you the time and effort involved in taking measurements over and over again.

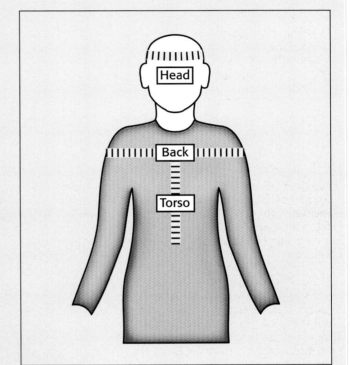

Estimate Stitch and Row Count

It's easy to determine how many stitches and rows you need for a project, and this information enables you to estimate how much yarn you require. You should purchase all of the yarn you need at the beginning of your project.

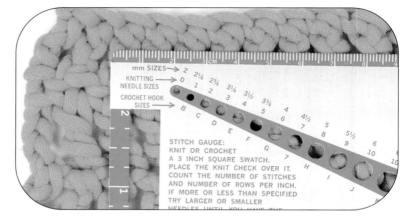

Estimate Stitch and Row Count

First, do a little math to figure out how many stitches and how many rows are required.

Sample Project: Scarf

6 inches wide x 60 inches long

① With the yarn you plan to use, work a 10 stitch x 10 row swatch. Measure and count how many stitches are in an inch.

② Multiply the number of stitches in an inch by the inches of width in the intended project.

For example, if your swatch has 4 stitches to an inch and your finished piece needs to be 6 inches wide, you'll need 24 stitches.

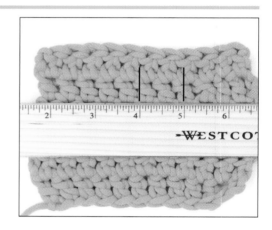

③ Measure and count how many rows are in an inch.

④ Multiply the number of rows in an inch by the inches of length in the intended project.

For example, if your swatch has 4 rows to an inch, and your finished piece needs to be 60 inches, you'll need to complete 240 rows.

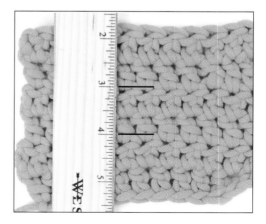

There is such a large variety of crochet stitches that figuring yardage for a project can be intimidating. Whatever the stitch pattern you choose, figuring out how much yarn you need isn't as hard as you think.

Estimate How Much Yarn You Need

Using the swatch you created on the preceding page:

1 Unravel the number of stitches equal to an inch. Measure the unraveled yarn.

For example: 4 stitches in the swatch = 4 inches of yarn.

2 Multiply this yarn length by the number of inches in the desired finished width of your project. This number is the length of yarn required to make 1 row.

For example, 4 inches of yarn x 6 inches of width in a row = 24 inches of yarn needed for 1 row.

3 Multiply the number of rows needed by the number of inches in a row.

For example, 24 inches x 240 rows = 5,760 inches.

4 Convert the inches to yards (36 inches = 1 yard). That's how much yarn you need.

When in doubt, purchase too much yarn. Keep in mind that your gauge may vary slightly throughout a project. You must also remember to account for the yarn tails you leave at the beginning and end of your work and every time you change color or add a new ball of yarn.

chapter 4

Basic Techniques

Now that you know the basic stitches, you're ready to move on to more adventurous crochet. In this chapter, you will learn how to shape your crochet pieces, work in the round, change colors, and finish off a project.

Increase

You use increases to add one or more stitches to a round or row. The pattern abbreviation for an increase is *INC* or *inc*.

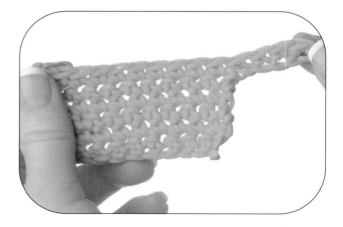

Increase at the Beginning of a Row

You use extra chains to provide room for more stitches at the end of a row.

1. At the end of the row before the increase: Work a chain stitch for each increase, plus the turning chain.

   Note: Refer to the section "Make a Turning Chain" in Chapter 3 for more information.

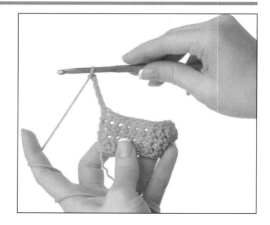

2. Turn your work. Skip the number of chains necessary for the turning chain. Work stitches into the extra chains.

3. Finish the row as usual.

   Note: To avoid mistakes, it's important to count the number of stitches in your rows. Doing so is especially important when increasing or decreasing.

Increase within a Row

Work multiple stitches into 1 stitch to create an increase within a row or round.

To increase by 1 stitch, work 2 stitches into a single stitch from the previous row.

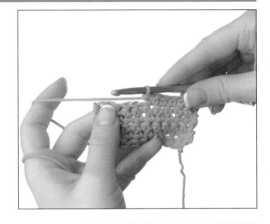

To increase by 3 stitches at once, work 4 stitches into a single stitch from the previous row.

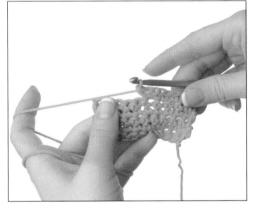

For a more subtle increase of 3 stitches, spread the increases out over multiple stitches:

1 Work 2 stitches into the stitch from the previous row.

2 Work 1 stitch into the next stitch from the previous row.

3 Work 2 stitches into the next stitch from the previous row. Work even across the rest of the row.

Note: "Work even" means to complete the row without changes in stitch pattern and without increasing or decreasing.

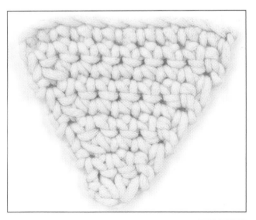

Decrease

You use decreases to reduce the number of stitches in a row. Doing so is useful in shaping crocheted fabric. There are several methods for decreasing; three are described below. The pattern abbreviation for a decrease is *DEC* or *dec*.

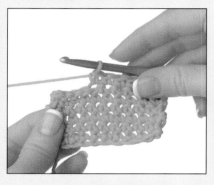

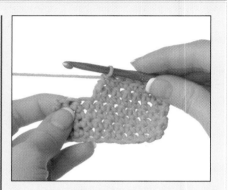

SKIP A STITCH

Skip the next stitch and work into the stitch after it as usual. This method decreases a row by one stitch but also creates a small hole. Many patterns use this method to create decorative holes in the fabric.

BEGINNING OF A ROW

Do not make a turning chain. Work a slip stitch (see Chapter 3) into each of the stitches from the previous row to be decreased. Make a turning chain necessary for the height of the row but do not turn. Continue with the row as usual. This creates a sharp decrease on one side. On the next row, do not work into the slip stitches.

END OF A ROW

At the end of a row, do not work the final number of stitches equal to the number to be decreased. Leave the proper number of stitches unworked, create your turning chain, and proceed to the next row.

Note: To decrease by 3 stitches, complete the row by working into the fourth stitch from the end.

Decrease Gradually by Working Stitches Together

You create a gradual decrease by working stitches together. You can use this flexible decrease method anywhere in a row. The pattern abbreviation for a gradual decrease is #TOG (with # replaced by the number of stitches to be worked together, as in 2TOG). Any number of stitches can be worked together, depending on the shaping effect you want.

Any type of stitch can be used for this type of decrease. We've used double crochet as an example here.

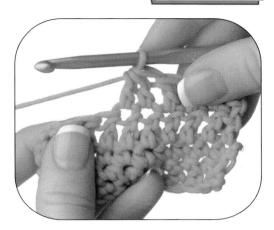

Work Stitches Together

1 Work the stitch as usual until the final step, when 2 loops remain on the hook. Do not complete the stitch.

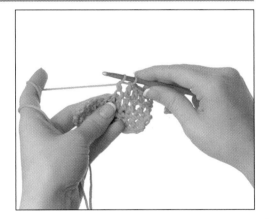

2 Insert the hook into the next stitch and work to the same point. There are now 4 loops on the hook. Yarn over and draw the yarn through all 4 loops.

The decrease you have created will look like 2 stitches sharing a top.

Note: *For a gradual decrease, use several 2TOGs worked throughout a row. For a sharper decrease, use a 3TOG or 4TOG.*

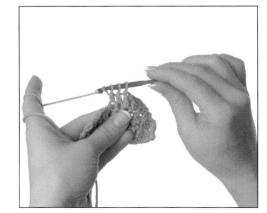

Create a Ring Using the Chain Stitch

You can use the chain stitch to create a ring as a foundation for working in the round.

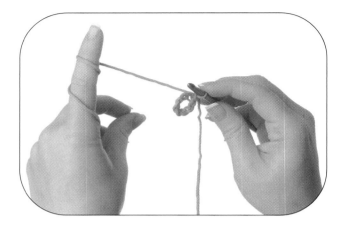

Chain Stitch

1 Chain 5 (a).

> **Note:** See the section "Make a Chain Stitch" in Chapter 3 for more on chains.

2 Slip stitch in the fifth chain from the hook (b).

> **Note:** See the section "Make a Slip Stitch" in Chapter 3 for more on slip stitch.

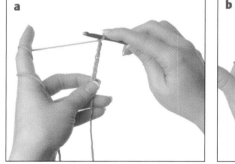

TIP

There are different ways to work into the ring:

1. Work into each chain as you would work into a foundation chain.
2. Ignore the chains and work through the center of the ring.

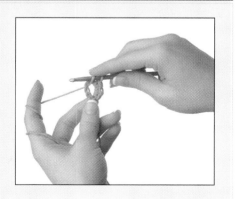

Using a loop to form your foundation for working in the round creates an invisible, adjustable ring. The first round of stitches is worked into the loop.

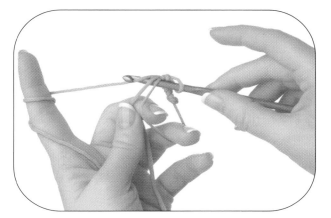

Loop

1 Make a slip knot, leaving a longer tail than usual. Place the slip knot on your hook.

2 Wrap the yarn tail twice around your two middle fingers to create the loop.

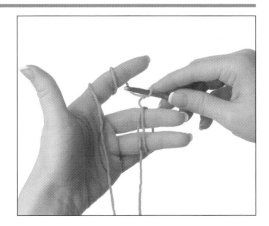

3 Insert your hook into the ring. Yarn over (a).

4 Draw the yarn through both the loop formed and the loop on the hook (b).

After you have worked the required number of stitches into the loop, pull the tail to tighten the loop.

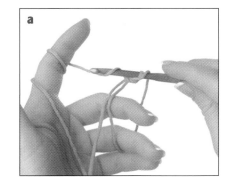

a

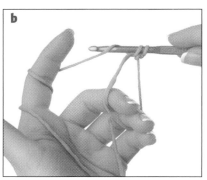

b

Work in the Round: Rounds

Make hats, baskets, flowers, and garments by working in the round. Use rows to create a round piece with an even, finished edge. The following instructions use single crochet, but any stitch can be used.

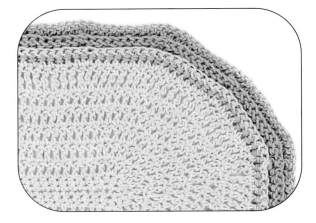

Rounds

To get started, choose one of the ring methods from the preceding sections.

1. Chain 1 to create a turning chain. Do not turn.

   Note: Just as you do when working in straight rows, you use turning chains at the beginning or end of a round to accommodate the height of your stitches. Unlike when working in rows, do not turn your work at the end of a round unless instructed to do so. Make a turning chain and continue working in the same direction.

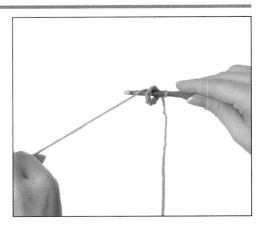

2. Work 6 single crochets into the ring.
3. Slip stitch into the top of the first single crochet of the round to join.

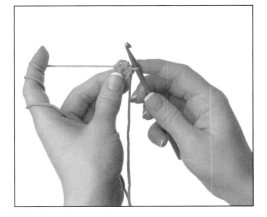

④ Chain 1. Work 2 single crochets into the first single crochet from the previous round.

⑤ Work 2 single crochets into each stitch in the round.

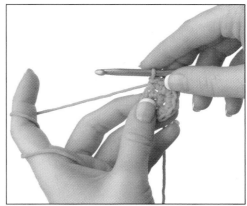

⑥ Slip stitch into the top of the first single crochet of the round to join.

There will be 10 single crochets in this round.

Note: See page 63 for details on shaping in the round.

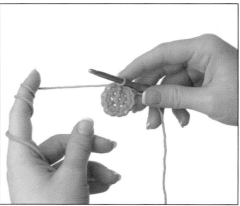

Work in the Round: Spiral Method

Work in the round without joining rows or making a turning chain by simply building on top of the last round without a turning chain.

The following instructions use single crochet, but you can use any stitch.

Spiral Method

To get started, choose one of the ring methods from the section "Create a Ring Using the Chain Stitch."

1. Work 6 single crochets into the ring (a).

2. Work 2 single crochets into each single crochet of the previous round (b). Mark the first single crochet in this round with a stitch marker or a scrap piece of yarn to help you keep track of where the round started. Move the marker with each new round.

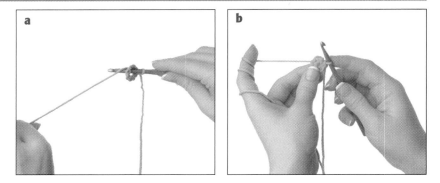

3. Continue to work 2 single crochets into each stitch of the round.

4. Work each round without joining with a slip stitch or creating a turning chain.

   Note: *See page 63 for details on shaping in the round.*

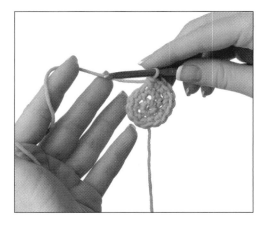

Shape in the Round: Gradual Increases

Evenly spaced increases create gradual shaping that is perfect for projects like hats.

Gradual, Spaced Increases

Continue from the final step on page 61 or page 62.

Increasing each row by the same number of stitches you started with is a good rule of thumb for creating gradual increases. Achieve this by interspersing increases with even work so that the number of increases you make are evenly distributed throughout the round.

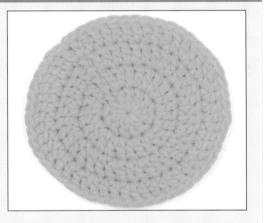

The following example is for a piece that starts with 6 stitches in the first round.

	Gradual, Spaced Increases		
Round	Total Number of Stitches after Increasing	Number of Increases	Number of Stitches between Increases
1	6	0	0
2	12	6	1
3	18	6	2
4	24	6	3

Refer to the hat pattern on page 242 to see this method in action.

Join a New Ball of Yarn and Change Color

Whether it's time to switch to a new ball of yarn because you are running out or because you simply want to change to a different color or texture, you can make the switch at any point in your crocheted piece.

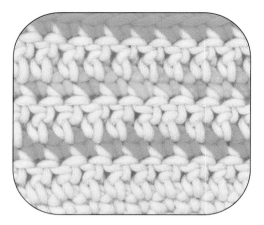

Join a New Ball at the End of a Row

This method creates a secure and nearly invisible yarn change, whether you are continuing in the same color or switching to a new color. It is excellent for crocheting stripes.

1 Work the final stitch of the row until only 2 loops remain on the hook. Do not complete the stitch.

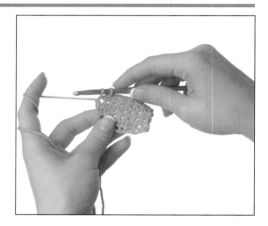

2 Yarn over with the *working yarn.*

The *working yarn* is the yarn you are working with, before switching.

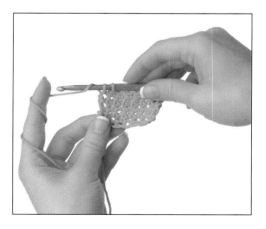

3 Yarn over with the new yarn. Leave a 6-inch tail hanging off the back of the hook.

4 Draw both yarns through the stitch (a).

5 Drop the old yarn. (You will weave in the tail later.) Make the appropriate turning chain with the new *working yarn* (b).

Note: *For more on weaving in ends, see the section "Weave in Yarn Tails."*

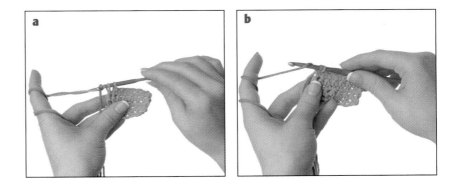

TIP

To work a yarn change in the middle of a row, follow steps 1–5. But, instead of making a turning chain, continue working across the row as normal.

Even though you have completed all the crochet stitches for your project, you still have work left to do! These finishing techniques will help you create a neat, finished-looking project.

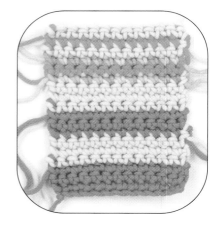

Fasten Off

Complete the last stitch. Cut the yarn, leaving a tail at least 6 inches long. Yarn over and draw the entire tail through the loop. Pull tight.

Now you're ready to weave in the tail or add a decorative edging. (See Chapter 11 for more on edgings.)

TIP

Sometimes a knot is necessary to keep the yarn securely fastened. Tie a simple knot before weaving in the tail.

Weave In Yarn Tails

Weaving in yarn tails is a necessary step in finishing any piece. Use a tapestry needle to weave yarn tails through the stitches.

To make sure the tail doesn't slip out, create a *U* or *C* shape as you sew the yarn into the wrong side of the crochet stitches. The *wrong side* of your work is the side that will not face out when the piece is completed. For example, the side of a garment that touches your skin is the wrong side.

1 Insert the needle into the body of the first stitch and draw the needle through.

2 Insert the needle into the next stitch (a).

3 Insert the needle into the next row (b).

4 Insert the needle into the next row.

5 Continue weaving in the tail, creating a horseshoe or zigzag shape. Take care to make the tail as inconspicuous as possible on the side of the work that will show (the *right side*).

6 When you are sure you've woven in enough that the tail won't slip out, tug on the crochet fabric in all directions. Doing so pulls more of the tail through the piece. If the tail is woven too tightly, it will pull out when the fabric is stretched.

chapter **5**

Stitch Variations

Variations on the basic crochet stitches create interesting textures and open up endless possibilities for even the simplest crochet work.

Make a Double Treble Crochet

The double treble crochet stitch (also known as a quadruple stitch) is extremely tall and is frequently used in combination with other stitches to create dramatic stitch patterns. Its pattern abbreviation is DTR or dtr.

Double Treble Crochet

Foundation chain: Create a chain equal to the number of stitches you require, plus 5. (See the section "Make a Foundation Chain" in Chapter 3 for more information.) Work your first DTR into the sixth chain from your hook.

1 Yarn over 3 times (a).

2 Insert the hook into the next stitch, yarn over, and draw the yarn through the stitch (b).

Five loops are now on the hook.

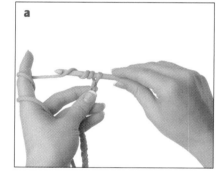

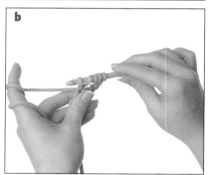

3 Yarn over and draw the yarn through the first 2 loops on the hook (a).

Four loops are now on the hook.

4 Yarn over and draw the yarn through the next 2 loops on the hook (b).

Three loops are now on the hook.

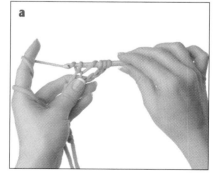

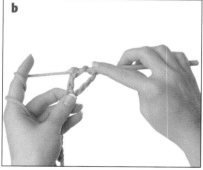

5 Yarn over and draw the yarn through the next 2 loops on the hook.

Two loops are now on the hook.

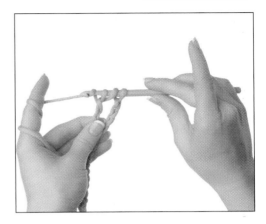

6 Yarn over and draw the yarn through both loops on the hook (a).

You have created 1 double treble crochet (b).

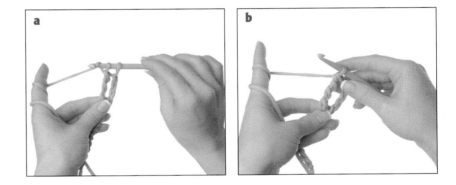

7 Continue to follow steps 1–6 until you have completed your first row of double treble crochet. Chain 5 to create a turning chain (a).

8 Turn the piece. Skip the first stitch at the beginning of the row. The turning chain counts as the first double treble crochet of the row. Follow steps 1–6 to create a double treble crochet in the second stitch of the row (b) and in each stitch thereafter.

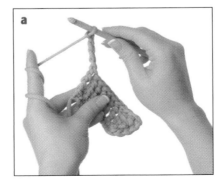

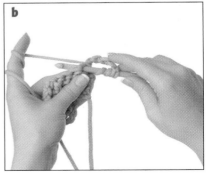

Make an Extended Single Crochet

The extended single crochet stitch is taller than the single crochet stitch. (See the section "Make a Single Crochet" in Chapter 3 for more information.) It creates an interesting texture that adds a change of pace to any project. Its pattern abbreviation is ESC or esc.

Extended Single Crochet

Foundation chain: Create a chain equal to the number of stitches you require, plus 2. (See the section "Make a Foundation Chain" in Chapter 3 for more information.) Work your first extended single crochet into the third chain from your hook.

1 Insert the hook into the next stitch, yarn over, and draw the yarn through the stitch.

Two loops are now on the hook.

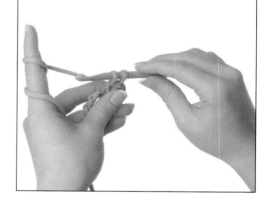

2 Yarn over and draw the yarn through the first loop on the hook.

Two loops are now on the hook.

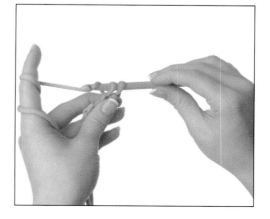

3 Yarn over and draw the yarn through both loops on the hook.

One loop is now on the hook.

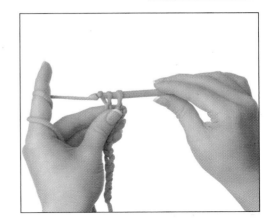

You have created 1 extended single crochet.

4 Repeat steps 1–3 until you have completed your first row of extended single crochet. Chain 2 to create a turning chain.

5 Turn the piece. Insert your hook through both loops at the top of the first stitch from the previous row. Repeat steps 1–3.

Make an Extended Double Crochet

The extended double crochet stitch is a taller variation of the standard double crochet. (See the section "Make a Double Crochet" in Chapter 3 for more information.) The abbreviation for the extended double crochet stitch is EDC or edc.

Extended Double Crochet

Foundation chain: Create a chain equal to the number of stitches you require, plus 3. (See "Make a Foundation Chain" in Chapter 3.) Work your first extended double crochet into the fourth chain from the hook.

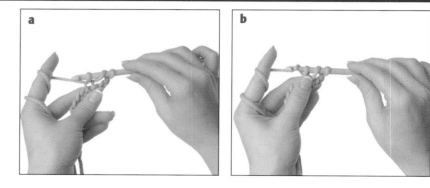

a

b

1 Yarn over once. Insert the hook into the next stitch, yarn over, and draw the yarn through the stitch (a).

Three loops are now on the hook.

2 Yarn over and draw the yarn through the first loop on the hook (b).

Three loops are now on the hook.

3 Yarn over and draw the yarn through 2 loops on the hook.

Two loops are now on the hook.

4 Yarn over and draw the yarn through the 2 remaining loops on the hook (a).

You have created 1 extended double crochet (b).

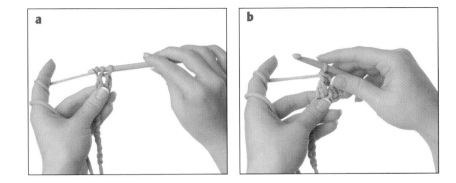

5 Continue to follow steps 1–4 until you have completed your first row of extended double crochet. Chain 3 to create a turning chain.

6 Turn the piece. Skip the first stitch at the beginning of the row. The turning chain counts as the first extended double crochet of the row. Follow steps 1–4 to create an extended double crochet in the second stitch of the row and in each stitch thereafter.

Note: Because the turning chain counts as the first extended double crochet at the beginning of a row, work into it as though it were an extended double crochet stitch.

Make an Extended Half Double Crochet

The extended half double crochet is a crochet stitch variation that's a bit taller than the standard half double crochet stitch. The abbreviation for the extended half double crochet stitch is **EHDC** or **ehdc**.

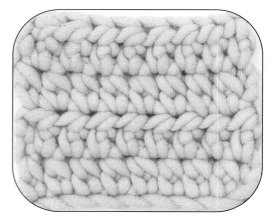

Extended Half Double Crochet

Foundation chain: Create a chain equal to the number of stitches you require, plus 2. (See "Make a Foundation Chain" in Chapter 3.) Work your first extended half double crochet into the third chain from your hook.

1 Yarn over once. Insert the hook into the next stitch, yarn over, and draw the yarn through the stitch.

Three loops are now on the hook (a).

2 Yarn over and draw the yarn through the first loop on the hook (b).

Three loops are now on the hook.

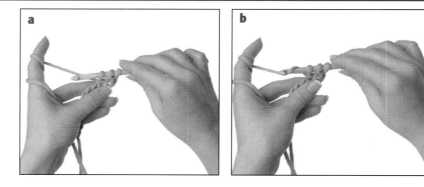

3 Yarn over and draw the yarn through all 3 loops on the hook.

One loop remains on the hook.

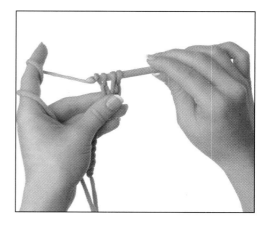

You have created 1 extended half double crochet.

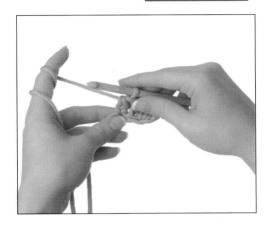

 Continue to repeat steps 1–3 until you have completed your first row of extended half double crochet. Chain 3 to create a turning chain (a).

5 Turn the piece. Skip the first stitch at the beginning of the row. The turning chain counts as the first extended half double crochet of the row. Follow steps 1–3 to create an extended half double crochet in the second stitch of the row and in each stitch thereafter (b).

TIP

Because the turning chain counts as the first extended half double crochet at the beginning of a row, you work into it as though it is an extended half double crochet stitch.

Make a Crab Stitch

The crab stitch (also known as the shrimp stitch, reverse single crochet, and corded reverse edging) is simple and decorative. Worked in reverse direction (from left to right if you are right-handed or right to left if you are left-handed), crab stitch is an easy stitch to make. Crab stitch does not have a pattern abbreviation but is frequently referred to as *rev sc* or *rsc*.

Crab Stitch

Note: *Because crab stitch is worked in reverse, begin with a foundation row of any stitch. Here, we use single crochet. (See "Make a Single Crochet" in Chapter 3.) Directions are for right-handers. Lefties, please reverse the direction.*

1 At the end of a row of any stitch, do not turn your work or make a turning chain. Insert your hook into the next stitch *to the right*.

2 Yarn over and draw the yarn through the stitch.

Two loops are now on the hook.

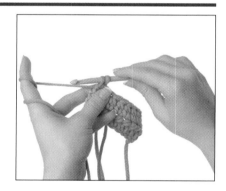

3 Draw the yarn through the 2 loops on your hook, the same way you would if you were working a single crochet.

You have made 1 crab stitch (a).

4 Continue to make crab stitches by inserting your hook into the next stitch to the right. When you reach the end of the row, do not turn your work (b).

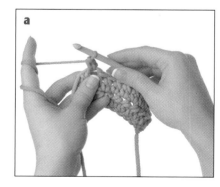

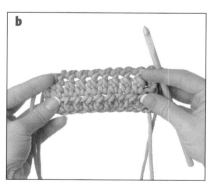

Crab stitch is most often used to create a simple and decorative border around a crocheted piece. You might see the stitch referred to as *reverse single crochet (rsc)*.

As mentioned in the section "Make a Crab Stitch," crab stitch is worked in reverse. Here, we give right-handed instructions for crab stitching a border around a swatch of single crochet, but you can place a border around a piece composed of any crochet stitch.

Crab Stitch Border

1 At the end of a row of any stitch, do not turn your work or make a turning chain. Follow steps 1–4 from the preceding section to work a crab stitch into each stitch along the top of your work (a).

2 Work 2 crab stitches into the corner stitch to turn the corner (b).

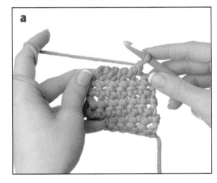

3 Work 1 crab stitch into each single crochet stitch along the right side of your work (a).

4 When you reach the next corner, work 2 crab stitches into the corner stitch and proceed to make 1 crab stitch in each stitch along the bottom. Do the same at the next corner and along the left side.

5 When you reach the top-left corner of your piece (b), fasten off and weave in the ends.

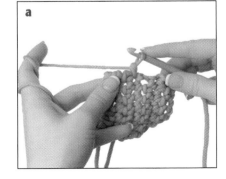

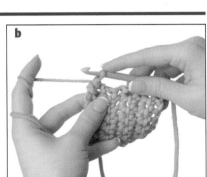

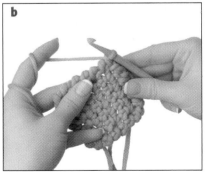

chapter 6

More Stitches

Venturing further into basic stitch variations opens up a world of textural possibilities.

Work in the Front Loop or Back Loop Only

Using texture in your crochet work creates variety and visual interest. In this section, learn the simplest technique to add a subtle texture to your basic stitches by working into only the front loops or back loops of stitches from the previous row.

Front Loop/Back Loop Texture Changes

Throughout this book, we instruct you to create stitches by inserting your hook into both loops of the stitch from the previous row, as shown here. You can also insert your hook into only the back or front loop when you work a stitch. Working into only one of the loops creates a subtle change in texture.

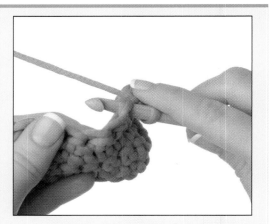

The *front loop* is the loop closest to you when you are holding your crochet work in front of you (a).

The *back loop* is the one farthest from you (b).

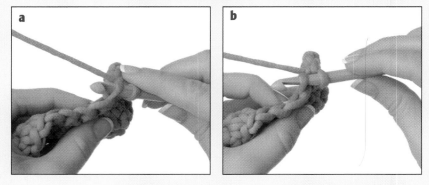

Crochet a swatch using any stitch. After working a few rows using both loops, crochet an entire row working into the front loop only (see photo). Note the slight ridge on one side of the fabric created by that unused back loop. Make another swatch working the back loop only.

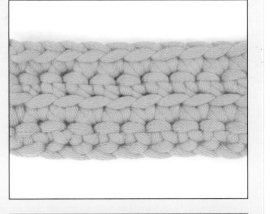

Alternating between working stitches into the front and back loops of the same row creates a rumpled texture.

Working into only one loop in every row for an entire piece creates a fabric with gentle drape. The fabric feels less dense than when both loops are worked.

Note: Patterns indicate whether to work in the front loop or back loop only; if no mention is made, work in both loops. Working into the front loop is also referred to as a front porch stitch, and working into the back loop as a back porch stitch.

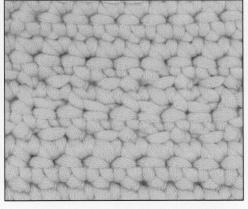

You can use spike stitches in a number of ways to add elaborate-looking details to crocheted fabric. Just work into any space below the top loops of the stitches from the previous row. This results in a "spike" of yarn connecting the stitch you have chosen to the current working row.

Spike Stitch

A spike stitch can be worked into fabric composed of any crochet stitch. This example uses single crochet. Begin with at least 2 rows of single crochet.

1 Insert your hook into the space directly below the stitch from the previous row.

Do not insert your hook into the top loops of the stitch.

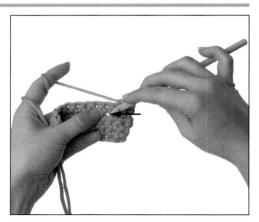

2 Yarn over and draw the yarn through the space. Pull this loop up to the working row, taking care not to pull the stitch too tight (a).

3 Yarn over and draw the yarn through both loops on the hook.

You have created 1 single crochet spike stitch (b).

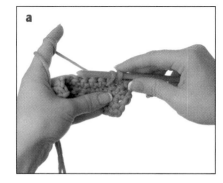

Spike stitches can be used in a variety of ways to add interest to your crochet work. Any of the following simple combinations can be used as a border or inside a piece.

WORK ALTERNATING SINGLE CROCHETS AND SPIKES

Alternate single crochets and spikes in the same row. This effect is striking as a border!

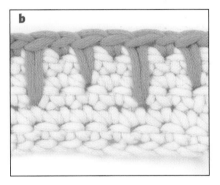

WORK LONG SPIKES

Work longer spikes by working into a space several rows below the working row. When drawing yarn through the space, be sure to make a nice long loop (a). Doing so prevents the fabric from buckling.

Combine single crochets with long spikes to add simple yet striking detail (b).

Work *1 SC, 1 long spike. Repeat from the * to the end of the row.

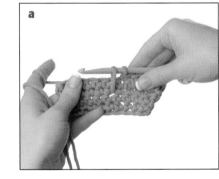

EXPERIMENT WITH COLOR

Changing color with each row, alternate working the following 2 spike rows with rows of single crochet between them. (See Chapter 4 for more on changing colors.)

Spike row 1: 1 single crochet, 1 spike, *3 single crochet, 1 spike. Repeat from the * to the end of the row.

Spike row 2: *3 single crochet, 1 spike. Repeat from * to the end of the row.

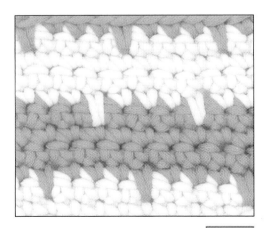

Make Crossed Stitches

You create crossed stitches by working pairs of stitches in backward order, creating a pattern of *X*s. Using treble crochet as an example, in this section you will learn a method for crossing stitches that can be used with any crochet stitch.

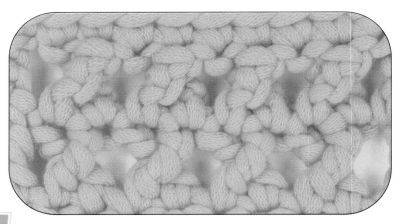

Make Rows of Crossed Treble Crochet

This stitch can be worked directly into a foundation chain or into any row of stitches. To make crossed treble crochet, start with a foundation chain of an odd number of stitches plus a turning chain of 4.

① Work a treble crochet into the sixth chain from the hook.

② Tilt the piece toward you and work a treble crochet into the chain preceding the last stitch made (see photo).

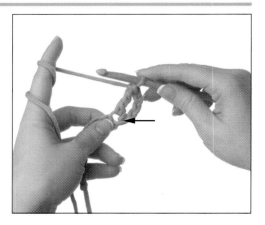

You have created a pair of crossed stitches.

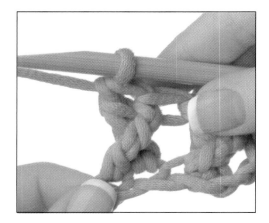

3 Skip 1 stitch and work a treble crochet into the next stitch.

4 Work a treble crochet into the skipped stitch preceding the last treble crochet made.

5 Repeat steps 3 and 4 until you have reached the last chain. Work a treble crochet into the last chain. Chain 4 and turn (a).

6 Skip the first stitch at the beginning of the row. The turning chain counts as a treble crochet. Repeat steps 3 and 4 until you have reached the last stitch. Work a treble crochet into the turning chain of the previous row. Chain 4 and turn (b).

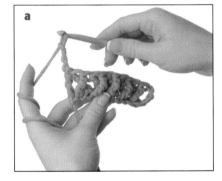
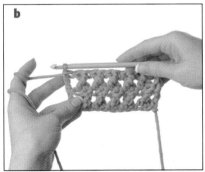

TIP

Any pair of crochet stitches can be crossed. You can also try placing chain stitches between each set of crossed pairs.

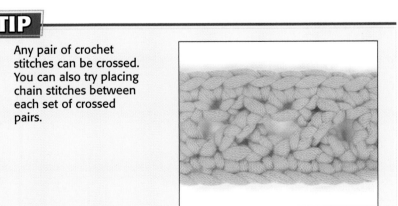

Work Double Crochet Post Stitches

Working around the front or back post of the stitch from the previous row offers another simple method to alter the texture of basic crochet stitches. This technique is often used to create ribs or cables. The post stitch is also known as a *raised stitch*.

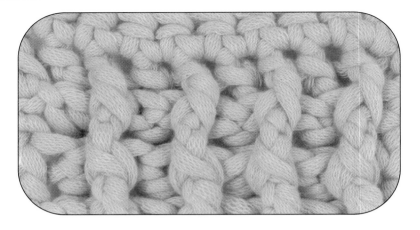

Front Post Double Crochet

Post stitches cannot be worked into the foundation chain; you must begin with a foundation row of any stitch. For this example, start with a row of double crochet. At the end of this foundation row, chain 2 for the turning chain and turn.

> **Note:** *Because a post stitch is shorter than a stitch worked into the top of another stitch, the turning chain for a post stitch is shorter by 1 chain.*

1 Yarn over once. Insert the hook from front to back to front around the post of the stitch in the previous row.

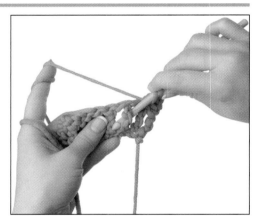

2 Yarn over and draw the yarn around the post (a). Complete the double crochet (b).

a
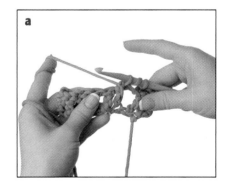

b
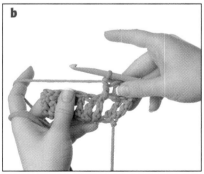

Back Post Double Crochet

For this example, start with a row of double crochet. At the end of this foundation row, chain 2 for the turning chain and turn.

 Yarn over once. Insert the hook from back to front to back around the post of the stitch in the previous row.

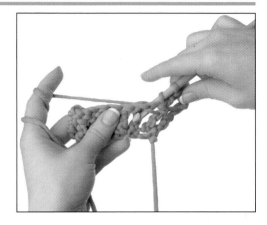

2 Yarn over and draw the yarn through. Complete the double crochet.

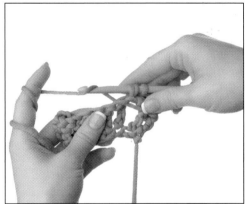

TIP

To create ribbing, use an even number of stitches. Begin by working a front post double crochet (FPDC) into the first stitch and a back post double crochet (BPDC) into the next stitch. Continue alternating front and back post stitches across the row. Make a turning chain and turn. Repeat this row to create a ribbed pattern.

Work a Treble Crochet Post Stitch

Work a treble crochet around the front or back post of a stitch from the previous row to create ribbing or other raised textures.

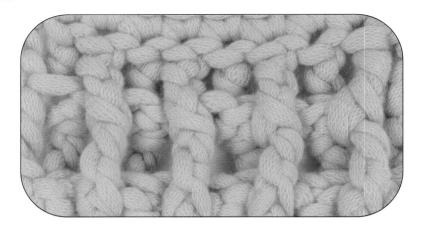

Front Post Treble Crochet

Post stitches cannot be worked into the foundation chain; for this example, begin with one row of treble crochet (a).

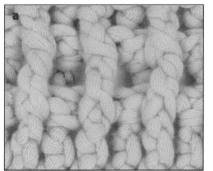

① Yarn over twice. Insert the hook from front to back to front around the post of the treble crochet stitch from the previous row (b).

② Yarn over and draw the yarn around the post. Complete the treble crochet.

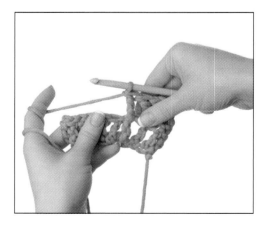

Back Post Treble Crochet

For this example, start with a row of treble crochet.

1 Yarn over twice. Insert the hook from back to front to back around the post of the stitch from the previous row.

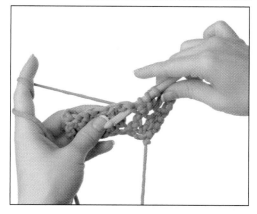

2 Yarn over and draw the yarn through (a). Complete the treble crochet (b).

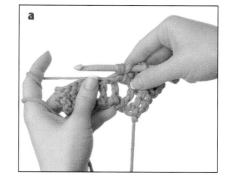

chapter 7

Combining Stitches

Now you're ready to combine the stitches you've learned to add another dimension to your crochet. Stitches can be combined, worked into the same space, or joined at their tops to create juicy, 3-D stitches. In this chapter, you can also try your hand at some step-by-step patterns as you learn.

Clusters

Clusters are in a category that includes a variety of stitch combinations, such as those worked together to create decreases, bobbles, and puffs. The stitches in a basic cluster are joined at the top and can be worked into one space or over several spaces.

See Chapter 4 for more on how to work stitches together to decrease.

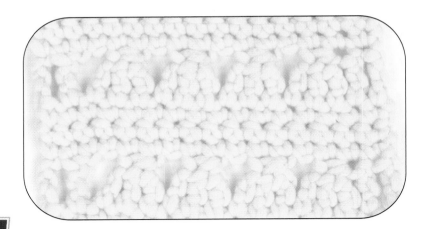

Make a Cluster with Treble Crochet

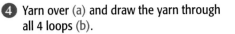

Note: *See the section "Make a Treble Crochet" in Chapter 3 for more information.*

1. Work a treble crochet until the final step, when 2 loops remain on the hook. Do not complete the stitch (see photo).

2. Insert the hook into the next stitch and work another treble crochet to the same point. There are now 3 loops on the hook.

3. Repeat step 2 to create a partial treble crochet stitch in the next stitch. There are now 3 partial treble crochets (4 loops) on the hook.

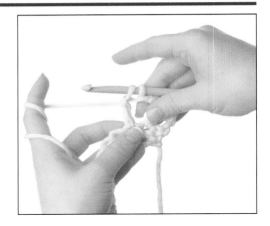

4. Yarn over (a) and draw the yarn through all 4 loops (b).

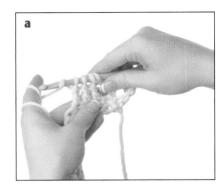

Work a Simple Treble Cluster Pattern

1 Row 1: Work 1 single crochet into second chain from hook. Work 1 single crochet into each chain across row, chain 4, and turn.

2 Row 2: Skip first stitch. The turning chain counts as first treble crochet of row. Work 1 treble crochet into next stitch. *Chain 2 and work 1 cluster of 3 treble crochet over next 3 stitches (a). Repeat from * until there are 2 stitches left to work in row. Chain 2. Work 1 treble crochet into each of last 2 stitches, chain 1, and turn (b).

3 Row 3: (See photo.) Work 1 single crochet into each of the first 2 stitches. *Work 2 single crochets into the chain space; work 2 single crochets into the space between the clusters. Repeat from the * until there are 2 stitches left to work in the row. Work 1 single crochet into each of the last 2 stitches, chain 1, and turn. (See photo.)

4 Row 4: Work 1 single crochet into each stitch across the row, chain 1 and turn.

5 Row 5: Work 1 single crochet into each stitch across the row, chain 4, and turn.

Repeat rows 2–5.

Note: *The foundation chain for the simple cluster pattern on the following page should be a multiple of 3 stitches plus 4 and 1 for the turning chain (for example, 12 + 4 = 16 + 1 = 17).*

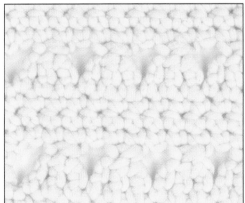

Bobbles

A cluster of tall stitches is worked into the same space and joined together at the top, creating a bobble that stands out. The bobble is a popular way to create playful textures.

Make a Bobble with Double Crochet

To create a bobble, stitches are worked together in the same manner as when making a decrease. (See Chapter 4 for more on how to work stitches together to decrease.)

1. Work a double crochet as usual until the final step, when 2 loops remain on the hook. Do not complete the stitch (a).

2. Insert the hook into the same stitch and work another double crochet to the same point. Four loops are now on the hook (b).

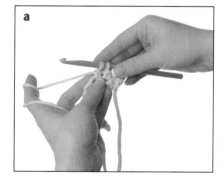
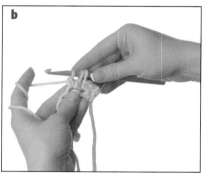

3. Repeat step 2 to create 2 more partial double crochet stitches. There are now 4 partial double crochets (5 loops) on the hook (a).

4. Yarn over and draw the yarn through all 5 loops.

5. Chain 1 to complete the stitch. You have made 1 bobble (b).

   Note: The foundation chain for the pattern on the next page should consist of an even number of stitches plus 1 for the turning chain (for example, 14 + 1 = 15).

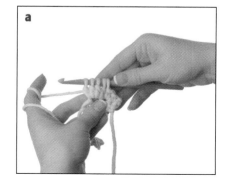
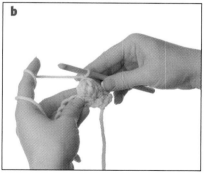

Work a Simple Bobble Pattern

1 Row 1: Work 1 single crochet into second chain from hook. Continue to work 1 single crochet into each chain across row. Chain 1 and turn.

2 Row 2: Work 1 single crochet into first stitch. *Work 1 single crochet into next stitch; work 1 bobble into next stitch (a). Repeat from * until 1 stitch remains. Work 1 single crochet into last stitch. Chain 1 and turn (b).

3 Row 3: Work 1 single crochet into each stitch across the row, chain 1, and turn.

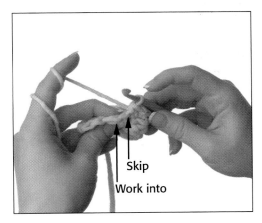

Note: *When working into the tops of bobble stitches, it looks like there are 2 stitches to work into. Skip the chain from the top of the bobble and work into the next stitch (see photo).*

Skip

Work into

4 Row 4: (a) Work 1 single crochet into the first stitch. *Work 1 bobble into the next stitch; work 1 single crochet into the next stitch. Repeat from the * until 1 stitch remains. Work 1 single crochet into the last stitch. Chain 1 and turn.

5 Row 5: Repeat row 3.

6 Repeat rows 2–5 (b).

Puffs

Puff stitches are bobbles worked with a half double crochet instead of a tall stitch. This results in the puff being shorter and puffier than a bobble.

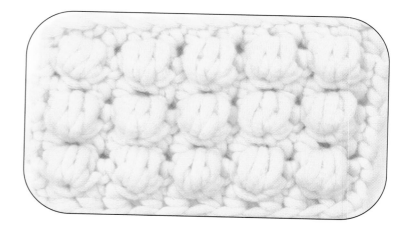

Make a Simple Puff

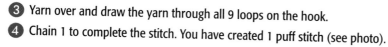

1 Yarn over once. Insert the hook into the next stitch, yarn over, and draw a long loop through the stitch. This loop should be looser than the loop normally created when working a half double crochet (a).

Note: *See the section "Make a Half Double Crochet" in Chapter 3 for more information.*

2 Repeat step 1 in the same stitch to create 3 more partial half double crochets (4 partial half double crochets in total).

Nine loops are now on the hook (b).

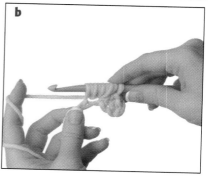

3 Yarn over and draw the yarn through all 9 loops on the hook.

4 Chain 1 to complete the stitch. You have created 1 puff stitch (see photo).

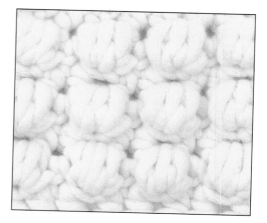

Work a Simple Puff Pattern

Try your hand at this simple puff pattern. Begin with a foundation chain with an odd number of stitches, plus 2 (for example, 13 + 2 = 15).

1 Row 1: Work 1 half double crochet into the third chain from the hook. Continue to work 1 half double crochet into each chain across the row, chain 1, and turn.

2 Row 2: Work 1 single crochet into first stitch of row. *Work a puff into next stitch. Work 1 single crochet into next stitch.* Repeat from * to * until 1 stitch remains. Work 1 single crochet into the last stitch (a). Chain 2 and turn.

3 Row 3: Work 1 half double crochet into the first stitch. *Skip the next stitch (the chain from the top of the puff stitch) (b). Work 1 half double crochet into each of the next 2 stitches.* Repeat from * to * to the end of the row. Chain 1 and turn.

Repeat rows 2 and 3.

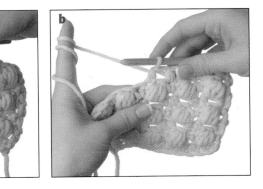

TIP

The texture and height of the puff stitch is determined by the length of the long loop in step 1.

Pulling the long loops can become more difficult as you begin to make the third partial HDC. Use your finger to pull it loose enough to match the other loops.

Popcorns

A popcorn consists of several tall stitches worked into the same space. Unlike a bobble, each stitch in a popcorn is worked to completion. The stitches are then gathered together in the final step.

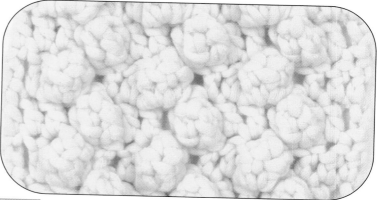

Make a Popcorn Using Four Double Crochets

Note: See the section "Make a Double Crochet" in Chapter 3 for more information.

1 Work a double crochet into the next stitch.

2 Work another double crochet into the same stitch (a).

3 Work 2 more double crochet stitches into the same stitch.

Four double crochets are now worked into 1 stitch.

4 Slip your hook out of the remaining loop (b).

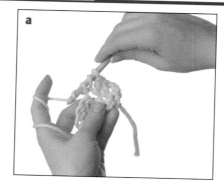
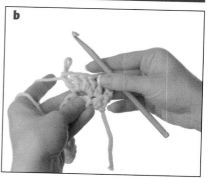

5 Insert your hook into the top of the first double crochet from this group and then into the empty loop.

Draw the empty loop through the top of that stitch and chain 1 to finish the popcorn.

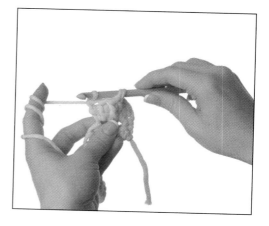

Work a Simple Popcorn Pattern

Try your hand at this simple popcorn pattern. The foundation chain for this pattern should be a multiple of 3 stitches plus 1 for the turning chain (for example: 12 + 1 = 13).

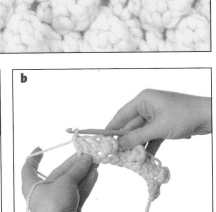

1 Row 1: Work 1 single crochet into the second chain from the hook. Continue to work 1 single crochet into each chain across the row. Chain 3 and turn.

2 Row 2: Skip the first stitch. (The turning chain counts as the first double crochet of the row.) Work 1 double crochet into the next stitch; work 1 popcorn into the next stitch (a). *Work 1 double crochet into each of the next 2 stitches; work 1 popcorn into the next stitch. Repeat from * until there are 3 stitches left to work in the row. Work 1 double crochet into each of the last 3 stitches. Chain 3 and turn (b).

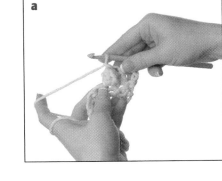

3 Row 3: Skip the first stitch. (The turning chain counts as the first double crochet of the row.) Work 1 double crochet into the next stitch; work 1 popcorn into the next stitch. *Work 1 double crochet into each of the next 2 stitches; work 1 popcorn into the next stitch. Repeat from the * until 1 stitch remains. Work 1 double crochet into the last stitch. Chain 3 and turn (a).

Repeat rows 2 and 3 (b).

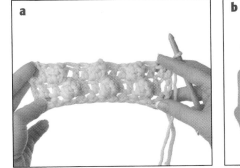

Bullions

The bullion stitch breaks from the standard format of most stitches. This stitch involves making many yarn overs (from 6 to 10, depending on the pattern) and has a texture all its own.

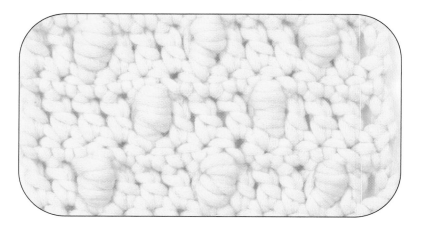

Make a Bullion Stitch

1. Yarn over 8 times.
2. Insert the hook in the next stitch, yarn over, and draw the yarn through the stitch (see photo). Yarn over.

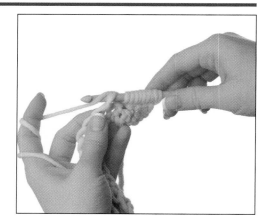

3. Draw the yarn over through all the loops on the hook.

   This can be tricky. Keep the yarn overs loose, and use your fingers to ease loops through one by one (a).

4. Yarn over and draw the yarn through the remaining loop on the hook. You have completed 1 bullion stitch (b).

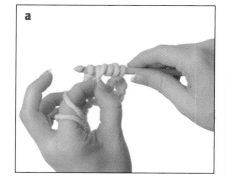

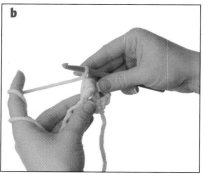

Work a Simple Bullion Pattern

1 Row 1: Work 1 single crochet into the second chain from the hook. Continue to work 1 single crochet into each chain across the row. Chain 3 and turn.

2 Row 2: Skip the first stitch. (The turning chain counts as the first double crochet of the row.) *Work 1 double crochet into each of the next 2 stitches; work 1 bullion into the next stitch (a). Repeat from the * until the last 3 stitches of the row. Work 1 double crochet into each of the last 3 stitches (b).

Repeat rows 1 and 2.

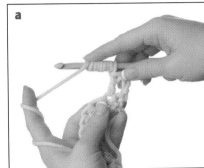

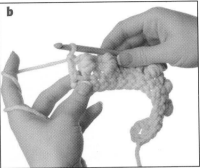

Follow a Pattern

Crochet patterns can look intimidating, but the information in this chapter will teach you how to navigate them with ease. Learn how to read crochet shorthand and how to figure your stitch and row gauge.

Knowing how to read a crochet pattern accurately enables you to make anything! In this section, learn about common pattern conventions.

Cloche

Add an eclectic feminine touch to the beanie pattern with this sweet edging.

Specifications

MATERIALS
1 hank Fleece Artist *Kid Silk* (70% kid/30% silk, 375 meters/250g) in Ruby Red
5.50 mm hook
Stitch marker

FINISHED SIZE
One size; 21î circumference, to fit average adult head

GAUGE
12 stitches and 13 rows = 4 inches (10 cm) in ESC

Make the Cloche

Round 1: Work 8 SC into the ring; sl st into the first SC to join the round. Gently pull on the tail to tighten the ring. Mark the first st with a stitch marker and CH 2 (8 SC total).
Round 2: Work 1 ESC into the same st the Sl st is worked into. *Work 2 ESC in the next SC. Repeat from * until 1 st remains. Remove marker. Work 1 ESC in the same st the first ESC was worked into; Sl st into the first ESC to join. Place marker in the first st. Continue to move the marker to indicate the first st of every round. CH 2 (16 ESC total).

Understand Pattern Conventions

ABBREVIATIONS

Crochet patterns are essentially step-by-step instructions for how to construct a finished piece. In the interest of fitting the greatest amount of instruction on one page, a fairly standard set of abbreviations is used for frequently occurring terms like stitch names, techniques, and instructions. Becoming familiar with these abbreviations enables you to effortlessly make sense of crochet shorthand. See the following section for a list of commonly used abbreviations.

GAUGE
12 stitches and 13 rows = 4 inches (10 cm) in ESC

Make the Cloche
Round 1: Work 8 SC into the ring; sl st into the first SC to join the round. Gently pull on the tail to tighten the ring. Mark the first st with a stitch marker and CH 2 (8 SC total).
Round 2: Work 1 ESC into the same st the Sl st is worked into. *Work 2 ESC in the next SC. Repeat from * until 1 st remains. Remove marker. Work 1 ESC in the same st the first ESC was worked into; Sl st into the first ESC to join. Place marker in the first st. Continue to move the marker to indicate the first st of every round. CH 2 (16 ESC total).
Round 3: Work 1 ESC into the same st the Sl st is worked into. Place a marker in the first st. Continue to move the marker to indicate the first st of every round. *Work 1 ESC into the next st and 2 ESC into the next st. Repeat from * until 1 st remains. Work 1 ESC into the next st. Work 1 ESC in the same st the first ESC was worked into; Sl st into the first ESC to join. CH 1. (24 ESC total)

SYNTAX

In the interest of brevity, crochet patterns often utilize the following devices to organize steps. With a bit of practice, you'll find that these devices make intricate patterns less wordy and easier to follow. Parentheses ( ) and brackets [ ] are used to group sections of instructions. Often, these symbols are used to indicate a certain number of stitches that are to be worked into the same stitch, as in:

Work [SC, CH 2, DC, CH2, SC] into next st.

Asterisks (*) are also used to group instructions. They indicate a set of instructions to be repeated a certain number of times, as in:

SC in first st, *DC in next st, CH 1, skip 1 st, SC in next st. Repeat from * to end of row.

In this case, you would continue to repeat the "double crochet in next stitch, chain 1, skip 1 stitch, single crochet in the next stitch" until you completed the row.

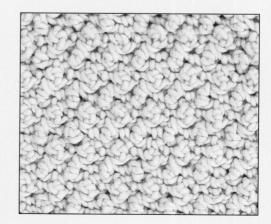

As we have mentioned, professionally produced crochet patterns usually utilize a set of fairly universal shorthand abbreviations to conserve space. The following is a list of commonly occurring abbreviations and what they stand for.

Crochet Abbreviations			
Abbreviation	**Meaning**	**Abbreviation**	**Meaning**
beg	beginning	lp	loop
bet	between	MC	main color
bl	back loop	patt st	pattern stitch
blo or BLO	work through the back loop only	pm	place marker
BPdc or BPDC	back post double crochet	prev	previous
BPtr or BPTR	back post treble (or triple) crochet	rem	remaining
CC	contrasting color	rep	repeat
ch or CH	chain	rev sc	reverse single crochet
ch-sp or CH SP	chain space	rnd	round
cont	continue	RS	right side
dc or DC	double crochet	sc or SC	single crochet
dec	decrease	sk	skip
dtr or DTR	double treble	sl st, SL ST, or SS	slip stitch
edc or EDC	extended double crochet	sp or SP	space
ehdc or EHDC	extended half double crochet	st or ST	stitch
esc or ESC	extended single crochet	tch or TCH or TC	turning chain
est	established	Tks	Tunisian knit stitch
fl	front loop	tog or TOG	together
flo or FLO	work through the front loop only	Tps	Tunisian purl stitch
FPdc or FPDC	front post double crochet	tr or TR	treble (or triple) crochet
FPtr or FPTR	front post treble (or triple) crochet	Tss	Tunisian simple stitch
hdc or HDC	half double crochet	WS	wrong side
hk	hook	yo or YO	yarn over
inc	increase		

Crochet patterns aren't as complicated as they might seem at first. This section gives you some tips for making sense of the shorthand and gaining the confidence to make sense of even the most complicated patterns.

At the top of a pattern, you will find information about sizing, materials, gauge, and stitch notes.

Cozy, Webby Sweater

This sweater is as cozy as it is contemporary. You use a large hook with two strands of DK-weight yarn to make a simple, webby lace. The body is worked in one piece, reducing the amount of seaming necessary. You add the collar along the front and neck after the body is complete.

Specifications

MATERIALS
10 (10, 12) balls South West Trading Company *Optimum DK* (154 yards/50g) in Silver
10 mm hook

TECHNIQUES USED
CH   Chain
SC   Single crochet
FLO   Front loop only
Using increases and decreases for shaping

FINISHED SIZE
Bust/Chest circumference S (M, L): 32–36 (38–42, 44–48)

Pattern Information

SIZING

The sizing of a garment is indicated with the smallest size followed by larger sizes in parentheses, as in:

Size: small (medium, large)

Chest measurement: 32"–36" (38"–42", 44"–48")

When the pattern calls for different instructions depending on size, those instructions are given in a similar fashion, with instructions for the first measurement followed by instructions for larger measurements in parentheses, as in:

Work 18 (20, 22) SC. CH 39 (39, 45, 45)

Sizing might not be indicated for some patterns, such as bags and scarves.

MATERIALS

Patterns specify which yarn is called for and how much of the yarn you need. They also tell you which hook size is recommended and what notions and embellishments you need, such as yarn needles, stitch markers, or buttons.

Specifications

MATERIALS
10 (10, 12) balls South West Trading Company *Optimum DK* (154 yards/50g) in Silver
10 mm hook

TECHNIQUES USED
CH   Chain
SC   Single crochet
FLO   Front loop only
Using increases and decreases for shaping

FINISHED SIZE
Bust/Chest circumference S (M, L): 32–36 (38–42, 44–48)

Get Started
You start this sweater at the bottom of the back of the body and build out from there.
CH 38 (44, 52).

GAUGE

Every pattern for which size is important (such as sweaters, slippers, and hats) includes information about the gauge on which the pattern is based. Always make a gauge swatch before beginning to work on such patterns so that you are sure to end up with the correct size. If your swatch is under or over gauge, adjust your hook size so that you obtain the correct gauge. (See the "Understanding Gauge" section for more information.) Use the gauge information given in the pattern to choose a yarn to substitute if you prefer not to use the yarn specified.

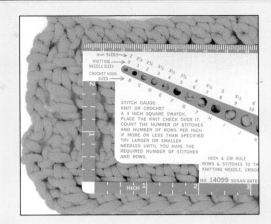

STITCH NOTES

Some patterns utilize stitch combinations that are complex or unique. Notes at the top of a pattern define the abbreviations that refer to these stitch combinations and give you the instructions once so that they don't have to be repeated throughout the pattern, as in:

Crossed DC: Sk 1 st, work 1 DC into the next st, work 1 DC into the skipped st.

TIP

A crochet pattern is like a recipe. Just follow the instructions one step at a time. You might find it helpful to read through the whole pattern before you begin so that you gain a better understanding of the project before you start. On the other hand, you might find the pattern less intimidating if you focus on one step at a time. Whichever way you choose, remember that the pattern is there to help you create something beautiful!

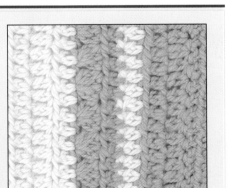

Understanding Gauge

For some projects, it's not crucial to create a finished piece to an exact size. For many other projects, however, exact size is imperative. An afghan can be a few inches off, but a few inches off in a sweater creates a garment that is neither useful nor flattering. A little bit of simple math is involved in making sure your finished garment will fit properly. Taking the time to ensure that your gauge is correct will save you from headaches and disappointment down the road.

Gauge

In crochet, *gauge* refers to the number of stitches or rows in a given length of fabric. For example, working a chunky weight yarn with an 8 mm hook might yield 9 single crochet **stitches** over 4 inches (10 cm). At the same time, it might yield 6 **rows** over 4 inches (10 cm).

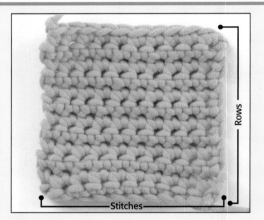

Every pattern you use should indicate the gauge required to create a finished piece of the proper dimensions. This information is located toward the beginning of the pattern.

It's important to work up a *gauge swatch* before you begin crocheting a project. If your swatch has too many rows or stitches within the area specified in the pattern, use a larger hook or adjust the number of stitches and/or rows you work. If your swatch has too few rows or stitches per the length specified, use a smaller hook or adjust the number worked. Continue to adjust your hook size until you attain the required gauge.

Note: See the following section, "Measure Your Gauge," for instructions on how to make and measure a gauge swatch.

Specifications

MATERIALS
1 hank Fleece Artist *Kid Silk* (70% kid/30% silk, 375 meters/250g) in Ruby Red
5.50 mm hook
Stitch marker

FINISHED SIZE
One size; 21" circumference, to fit average adult head

GAUGE
12 stitches and 13 rows = 4 inches (10 cm) in ESC

Make the Cloche
Round 1: Work 8 SC into the ring; sl st into the first SC to join the round. Gently pull on the tail to tighten the ring. Mark the first st with a stitch marker and CH 2 (8 SC total).
Round 2: Work 1 ESC into the same st the Sl st is worked into. *Work 2 ESC in the next SC. Repeat from * until 1 st remains. Remove marker. Work 1 ESC in the same st the first ESC was worked into; Sl st into the first ESC to join. Place marker in the first st. Continue to move the marker to indicate the first st of every round. CH 2 (16 ESC total).

Knowing the number of rows that fit in a given length of fabric is extremely important. If your row gauge is off from the required gauge in the pattern you are following, add or subtract rows to ensure a proper fit.

Knowing the number of stitches that fit in a given length of fabric is important, too. In this section, you will learn how to use this information to ensure that your finished project will be the proper size.

Use a Gauge Swatch to Measure Gauge

MAKE A SWATCH

1 Using the same yarn and hook you plan to use for your project, chain 28 (24, 20, 16, 12) stitches.

> **Note:** *Instructions given for sport weight (DK, worsted, bulky, super bulky) yarn.*

2 Work 24 (22, 18, 14, 10) rows in the same stitch or stitch pattern mentioned in the gauge section of your pattern. Tie off.

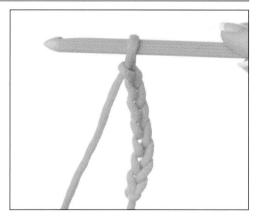

You should end up with a swatch that's approximately 4 inches square. Don't worry if your swatch isn't exactly this size.

> **Note:** *If you are using a natural fiber yarn, wash and block your swatch before measuring your gauge. Doing so ensures that your finished project will be the proper size after it's washed. (See Chapter 11 for more on blocking.)*

CONTINUED ON NEXT PAGE

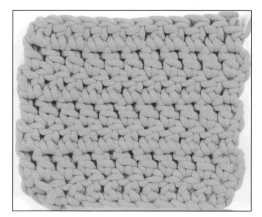

COUNT THE ROWS

1 Using a ruler, measuring tape, or gauge tool, count the number of rows in 4 inches.

Do not round up or down. If a row is cut off at the 4-inch point, count it as half a row.

2 Make a note of this number.

***Note:** It is common for crocheters to be more concerned about attaining the proper stitch gauge, because adjusting a pattern to accommodate a different stitch gauge is generally more complicated than adjusting for a different row gauge. If your row gauge is off by a small amount, you can adjust by crocheting slightly more or fewer rows in your piece.*

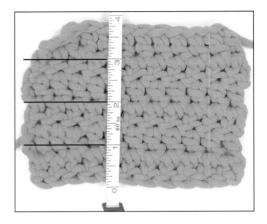

COUNT THE STITCHES

1 Using a ruler, measuring tape, or gauge tool, count the number of stitches in 4 inches.

Do not round up or down. If a stitch is cut off at the 4-inch point, count it as half a stitch.

2 Make a note of this number.

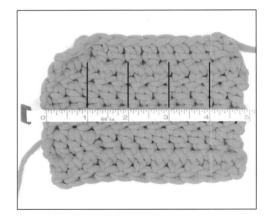

ADJUST IF NECESSARY

- If the number of stitches you crocheted over 4 inches is higher than the number required by the pattern you're following, use a larger hook to make a new swatch. Continue to increase your hook size until you create a swatch with the proper gauge. If you need to go up more than a couple of hook sizes, you might want to consider switching to a yarn of a heavier weight.

- If the number of stitches you crocheted over 4 inches is lower than the number required by the pattern, use a smaller hook to make a new swatch. If you need to go down more than a couple of hook sizes, you might want to consider using a lighter weight yarn.

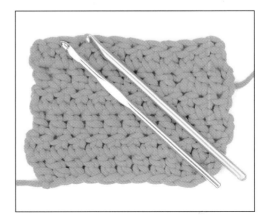

Our discussion of how to read crochet patterns has focused on how to make sense of crochet short-hand. Some patterns, however—especially those published in Europe and Asia—utilize stitch symbols to convey crochet instructions. Each stitch or stitch cluster is represented by a symbol. Use this chart to determine what each symbol represents.

chain stitch (**ch**)	⌒	V-stitch (**V-st**)	
slip stitch (**sl st**)	• OR ➤	crossed double crochet (**crossed dc**)	OR
single crochet (**sc**)	✕ OR ＋	shell [of 4 dc]	
half double crochet (**hdc**)		picot [of ch 3, sl st]	
double crochet (**dc**)		cluster [of 4 dc]	
triple crochet (**tr**)		reverse [sc]	
double triple crochet (**dtr**)		puff st [of 3 dc]	
triple triple crochet (**trtr**)		popcorn (**pop** or **pc**) [of 5 dc]	
single crochet in front loop only (**flp**)	✕	bobble [composed of 5 loops]	
single crochet in back loop only (**blp**)	✕	loop stitch (**loop st**)	
front post double crochet (**FP dc**)		long stitch (**long st**) or spike	
back post double crochet (**BP dc**)			

9

Stitch Patterns

This chapter contains several simple stitch patterns. You can use these patterns in any of your projects to add texture and visual interest. Use them as inspiration to experiment with stitch patterns of your own. Play with fibers and colors to create truly unique fabrics. To ease your introduction to reading patterns, read both the "formal" pattern and the "plain English" explanation that appears below it.

Mesh Fabric Using Crochet Arches

Mesh is the simplest form of crocheted lace. You use chains connected by single crochet stitches to create an open, versatile piece.

Here are two versions of the same pattern. One is written in abbreviated form, and the other is in "plain English."

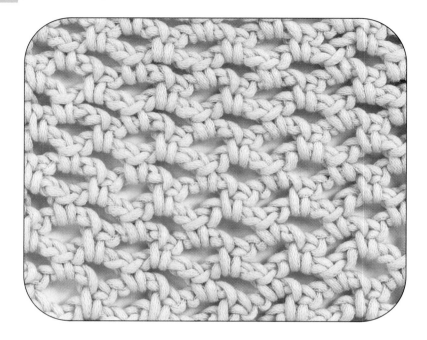

The Pattern

Row 1: SC into fifth CH from hook, *CH 3, skip 2 CHs, and SC into next CH. Repeat from * to end of row. CH 4 and turn.

Row 2: SC into next CH space. *CH 3 and SC into next CH space. Repeat from * to complete row.

Repeat row 2 to desired length.

The Pattern in Plain English

Create a foundation chain that is a multiple of 3 stitches plus 1.

1 Row 1: Work 1 single crochet into the fourth chain from the hook. (The first 3 chains count as the first arch.)

2 *Chain 3. Leaving the next 2 chains unworked, make a single crochet into the next chain (a).

3 Repeat from the * to the end of the row. When the row is complete, chain 3 (b) and turn.

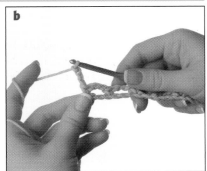

4 Row 2: Work 1 single crochet into the first space created by chains from the previous row. To work into a *chain space,* insert your hook into the space, yarn over, and draw the yarn through the space (a), yarn over, draw the yarn through both loops (one single crochet completed).

5 *Chain 3 and work 1 single crochet into the next chain space. Repeat form the * until you have worked a single crochet into the last chain space of the row. Chain 3 and turn (b).

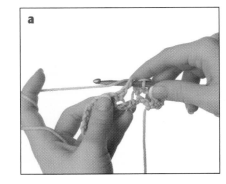
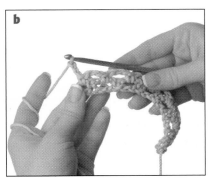

TIP

Also known as a trellis pattern, this simple format makes it very easy to create a loose, mesh fabric. You can vary the type of mesh you create by changing one or more aspects of this pattern:

- Increase the number of chains in each arch, but don't increase the number of skipped stitches.

- Increase the number of chains and skipped stitches.

- Use a taller stitch in place of the single crochet.

Crumpled Stitch Pattern

Alternating a short stitch with a tall stitch creates a soft, slightly rumpled texture. Use this stitch pattern to add style to a simple project.

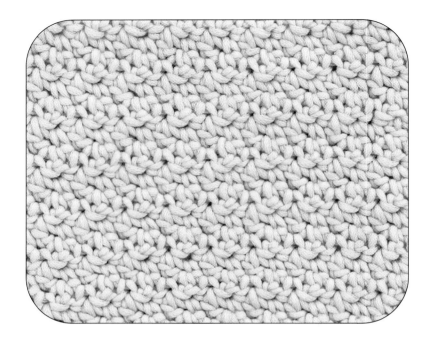

The Pattern

Row 1: SC into second CH from hook. *DC into next CH and SC into next CH. Repeat from * to last st of row. DC into last st, CH 1, and turn.

Row 2: SC into first st, *DC into next st, and SC into next st. Repeat from * to last st of row. DC into last st, CH 1, and turn.

Repeat row 2.

The Pattern in Plain English

The foundation chain for this pattern consists of an even number plus 1 for the turning chain.

1. Row 1: Work 1 single crochet into the second chain from the hook. *Work 1 double crochet into the next chain. Work 1 single crochet into the next chain. Repeat from the * across the row to the last chain, and work 1 double crochet into the last chain. Chain 1 and turn.

2. Row 2: Work 1 single crochet into the first stitch. *Work 1 double crochet into the next stitch. Work 1 single crochet into the next stitch. Repeat from the * across the row to the last stitch, and work 1 double crochet into the last stitch. Chain 1 and turn.

3. Repeat row 2.

   Notice that you work single crochet stitches into the double crochet stitches of the previous row, and vice versa.

Crunch Pattern

Combining half double crochets with slip stitches creates a dense fabric with an interesting texture. Try using this stitch pattern for hats or purses.

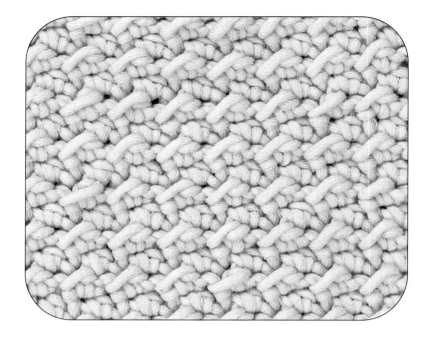

The Pattern

Row 1: Sl st into second CH from hook. *HDC into next CH. Sl st into next CH. Repeat from * to last st of row. HDC into last st, CH 1, and turn.

Row 2: Sl st into first st. *HDC into next st. Sl st into next st. Repeat from * to last st of row. HDC into last st, CH 1, and turn.

Repeat row 2.

The foundation chain for this pattern consists of an even number plus 1 for the turning chain.

1 Row 1: Work 1 slip stitch into the second chain from the hook. *Work 1 half double crochet into the next chain. Work 1 slip stitch into the next chain.

2 Repeat from the * across the row to the last chain. Work 1 half double crochet into the last chain, chain 1, and turn.

3 Row 2: Work 1 slip stitch into the first stitch, *Work 1 half double crochet into the next stitch. Work 1 slip stitch into the next stitch. Repeat from the * across the row to the last stitch. Work 1 half double crochet into the last stitch, chain 1, and turn.

4 Repeat row 2.

TIP

Notice that you work slip stitches into the half double crochet stitches of the previous row and vice versa.

Crunchy Dots Pattern

Placing a tall treble crochet stitch between two single crochet stitches forces the tall stitch to fold on itself and pouf out. This pattern creates a fun, three-dimensional fabric.

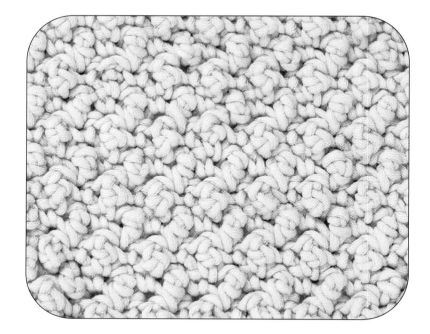

The Pattern

Row 1: SC into second CH from hook. *SC into next CH, and TR into next CH. Repeat from * across to last CH. SC into last CH, CH 1, and turn.

Row 2: SC into first st. *SC into next st and TR into next st. Repeat from * to last st of row. SC into last st, CH 1, and turn.

The foundation chain for this pattern consists of an even number plus 1 for the turning chain.

1 **Row 1:** Work 1 single crochet into the second chain from the hook. *Work 1 single crochet into the next chain, and work 1 treble crochet into the next chain. Repeat from the * across to the last chain. Work 1 single crochet into the last chain. Chain 1 and turn.

2 **Row 2:** Work 1 single crochet into the first stitch. *Work 1 single crochet into the next stitch. Work 1 treble crochet into the next stitch.

3 Repeat from the * across the row to the last stitch. Work 1 single crochet into the last stitch, chain 1, and turn.

4 Repeat row 2.

Note: The treble stitches will likely fold and pouf away from you as you work the row. On every other row, use your finger to push the treble through so that it poufs toward you. This way all the trebles pouf out on the same side.

Granite Stitch Pattern

Alternating chain stitches with single crochet stitches results in a woven effect that makes a lovely fabric with excellent drape.

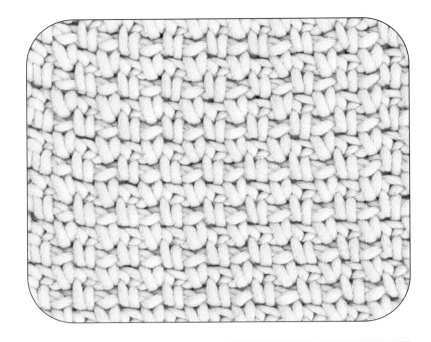

The Pattern

Row 1: SC into second CH from hook. *SC, CH 1, and skip 1 CH. Repeat from * to last 2 CHs. CH 1 and skip 1 CH. SC into last CH. CH 1, and turn.

Row 2: SC into first st. *SC into CH space, CH 1, and skip 1 st. Repeat from * to last 2 sts of row. CH 1, skip 1 st, and SC into last st. CH 1 and turn.

Repeat row 2.

The Pattern in Plain English

The foundation chain for this pattern consists of an even number plus 1 for the turning chain.

1 Row 1: Work 1 single crochet into the second chain from the hook. *Work 1 single crochet into the next chain, chain 1, and skip 1 chain.

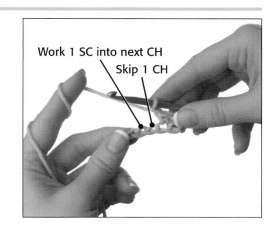

Work 1 SC into next CH
Skip 1 CH

2 Repeat from the * until 2 chains remain. Chain 1, skip 1 chain, and work 1 single crochet into the last chain. Chain 1 and turn.

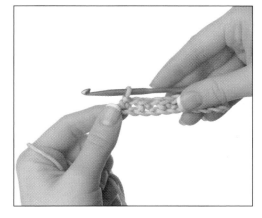

3 Row 2: Work 1 single crochet into the first stitch. *Work 1 single crochet into the next chain space, chain 1, and skip 1 stitch. Repeat from the * to the end of the row. Work 1 single crochet into the last stitch. Chain 1 and turn.

Trinity Pattern

Use the trinity cluster stitch to create an elegantly textured fabric that you can use either for the body of a work or as a decorative detail. First we explain how to make the stitch, and then we tell you how to create the pattern.

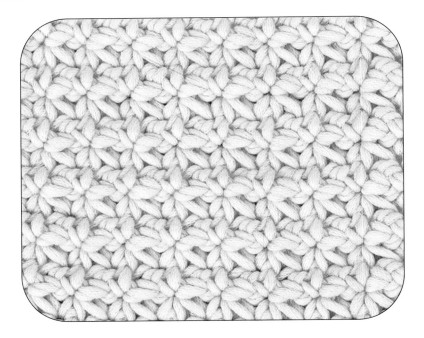

The Trinity Cluster Stitch

1. Insert the hook into the same space as the last st, yarn over, and draw the yarn through.
2. Insert the hook into the next stitch, yarn over, and draw the yarn through. Then insert your hook into the next stitch, yarn over, and draw the yarn through. (See photo on opposite page.)
3. Yarn over and draw the yarn through all 4 loops.

The Pattern

Row 1: SC into second CH from hook. SC into each CH across, CH 1, and turn.

Row 2: SC into first st. Work 1 trinity cluster, *CH 1, and work 1 trinity cluster (working first stitch of cluster into same space as the previous stitch). Repeat from * across row. Work 1 SC into space of last trinity cluster, CH 1, and turn.

Repeat row 2.

The foundation chain for this pattern consists of an even number plus 1 for the turning chain.

1 Row 1: Work 1 single crochet into the second chain from the hook. Continue to work 1 single crochet into each chain across the row. Chain 1 and turn.

2 Row 2: Work 1 single crochet into the first stitch. Work 1 trinity cluster, working the first stitch of the cluster into the same stitch as the single crochet, and then into the next 2 stitches.

3 *Chain 1. Work 1 trinity cluster into the same space as the last stitch of the previous cluster, and then into the next 2 stitches.

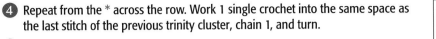

4 Repeat from the * across the row. Work 1 single crochet into the same space as the last stitch of the previous trinity cluster, chain 1, and turn.

5 Repeat row 2.

Chevron Pattern

Chevrons create a wavy fabric that is especially popular in baby blankets, afghans, and scarves. You shape this chevron by working three stitches into one stitch to create a chevron point.

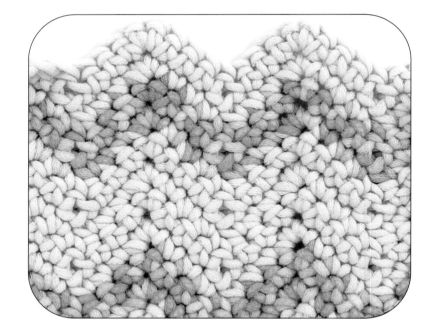

The Pattern

Row 1: 2 SC into second CH from hook. *1 SC into each of the next 3 CHs. Skip next 3 CHs. 1 SC into each of the next 3 CHs. 3 SC into next CH and 1 SC into each of the next 3 CHs. Repeat from * to end of row. 2 SC into final CH. CH 1 and turn.

Row 2: 2 SC into the first st. *3 SC, skip 2 sts, 3 SC, and 3 SC into next st. Repeat from * to end of row. 2 SC into last st. CH 1 and turn.

Repeat row 2 to desired length.

The Pattern in Plain English

The foundation chain for this pattern consists of a multiple of 10 plus 1, plus 1 for the turning chain (for example, 30 + 1 + 1 = 32).

① Row 1: Work 2 single crochets into the second chain from the hook. *Work 1 single crochet into each of the next 3 chains. Leave 3 chains unworked (a).

② Work 1 single crochet into each of the next 3 chains. This creates a point and a bend in the row (b).

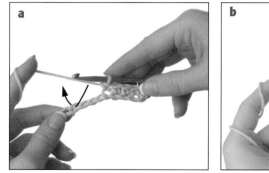

3 Work 3 single crochets into the next stitch. Working 3 single crochets into the first stitch bends the row. Work 1 single crochet into each of the next 3 chains.

4 Repeat from the * until the end of the row. Work 2 single crochets into the last stitch. Chain 1 and turn.

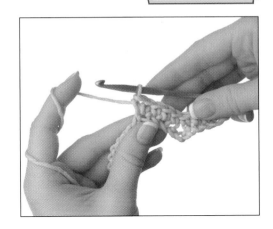

5 Row 2: Work 2 single crochets into the first stitch. *Work 1 single crochet into each of the next 3 stitches. Leave 2 stitches unworked. This builds the bend started in the previous row. Work 1 single crochet into each of the next 3 stitches. Work 3 single crochets into the next stitch—this stitch is the top of the bend created in the previous row. Repeat from the * to complete the row. Work 2 single crochets into the last stitch, chain 1, and turn.

6 Repeat row 2.

Note: See Chapter 4 for instructions on how to add colors to this pattern.

TIP

This pattern uses three single crochets between each curve. To vary this chevron pattern, simply add more single crochet stitch spaces between the curves. Adjust the length of your foundation chain accordingly.

For example, to change the pattern to 6 single crochets between each curve, you need a foundation chain with a multiple of 16 plus 1, plus 1.

Shells with Double Crochet

By working several stitches into one space, you can create a shell or fan. There are infinite varieties of shell patterns; this simple double crochet shell looks lovely in feminine garments or as a simple edging.

The Pattern

Row 1: SC into second CH from hook. SC into each CH across, CH 1, and turn.

Row 2: SC into the first st. Skip 2 sts, * 5 DC into the next st. Skip 2 sts, and SC into the next st. Repeat from * to end of row. CH 3 and turn.

Row 3: The turning CH counts as 1 DC. 2 DC into first st, *1 SC into middle DC of shell from previous row, 5 DC into next SC. Repeat from * to last st. Work 3 DC in last st, CH 1, and turn.

Repeat rows 2 and 3.

The Pattern in Plain English

The foundation chain for this pattern consists of a multiple of 6 plus 1 for the turning chain (for example 4 x 6 = 24 + 1 = 25).

① Row 1: Work 1 single crochet into the second chain from the hook. Continue to work 1 single crochet into each chain across, chain 1, and turn.

② Row 2: Work 1 single crochet into the first stitch. *Skip the next 2 stitches, work 5 double crochets into the next stitch, skip 2 stitches, and work 1 single crochet into the next stitch.

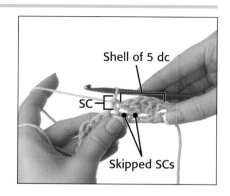

Shell of 5 dc

SC

Skipped SCs

3 Repeat from the * to the end of the row (a). Chain 3 and turn.

4 Row 3: The turning chain counts as the first double crochet of the row. Work 2 more double crochets into the first stitch (b). (This creates a half shell.)

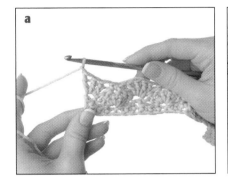

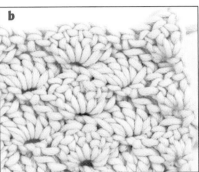

5 *Work 1 single crochet into the middle double crochet in the shell from the previous row.

6 Work 5 double crochets into the next single crochet.

7 Repeat from the * to the last stitch of the row. Work 3 double crochets into the last stitch, chain 1, and turn.

8 Repeat rows 2 and 3.

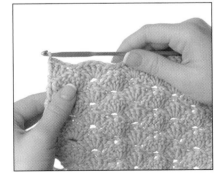

Odd Shells Pattern

Lacy and open, this stitch pattern uses V-stitches to create a variation on the basic shell pattern. Use it in similar projects, or experiment with new uses!

Combinations Used in This Pattern

V-stitch: Work [1 double crochet, chain 2, 1 double crochet] into the same stitch (a).

Odd V-stitch: Work [2 double crochets, chain 2, 1 double crochet] into the same st (b).

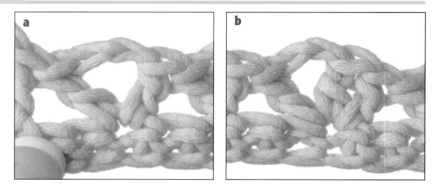

The Pattern

Row 1: SC into second CH from hook. SC into each CH across. CH 3 and turn.

Row 2: *V-st into second st, sk 2 sts, and work 1 odd V-st into next st. Repeat from * to last 3 sts. Skip 2 sts and DC into last st. CH 3 and turn.

Row 3: *1 odd V-st into CH 2 space, and 1 V-st into next CH 2 space. Repeat from * to end of row. 1 DC into space between turning CH and DC of the previous row. CH 3 and turn.

Row 4: *1 V-st into CH 2 space. Work 1 odd V-st into next CH 2 space. Repeat from * to end of row. 1 DC into space between turning CH and DC of previous row. CH 3 and turn.

The foundation chain for this pattern consists of a multiple of 8 plus 2, plus 1 for the turning chain (for example, 24 + 2 + 1 = 27).

1 Row 1: Work 1 single crochet into the second chain from the hook. Continue to work 1 single crochet into each chain across. Chain 3 and turn.

2 Row 2: Starting in the second stitch of the row, *work 1 V-stitch. Skip 2 stitches, and work 1 odd V-stitch into the next stitch. Repeat from the * across the row until 3 stitches remain. Skip 2 stitches and work 1 double crochet into the last stitch. Chain 3 and turn.

3 Row 3: Starting in the first chain 2 space, *work 1 odd V-stitch into the chain 2 space, and work 1 V-stitch into the next chain 2 space. Repeat from the *, working into each chain 2 space across the row. Work 1 double crochet into the space between the turning chain and double crochet from the previous row. Chain 3 and turn.

4 Row 4: Starting with the first chain 2 space: *Work 1 V-stitch into the chain 2 space and work 1 odd V-stitch into the next chain 2 space. Repeat from the *, working into each chain 2 space across the row. Work 1 double crochet into the space between the turning chain and double crochet of the previous row. Chain 3 and turn.

5 Repeat rows 3 and 4.

Popcorn Dance Pattern

A popcorn stitch is worked into this lively variation of the odd shells pattern. This pattern creates open fabric with excellent drape, or a great edging.

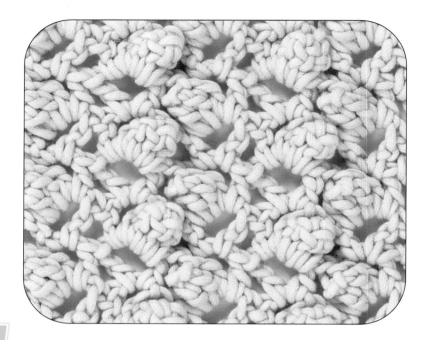

Combinations Used in This Pattern

V-stitch: Work 1 double crochet, chain 2, and 1 double crochet all into the same stitch (a).

Popcorn stitch: Work 4 double crochets into the same stitch. Join through the top and chain 1 (b). (See the section "Popcorns" in Chapter 7 for more information.)

Popcorn V-stitch: Work 1 double crochet, chain 2, and work 1 popcorn stitch all into the same stitch.

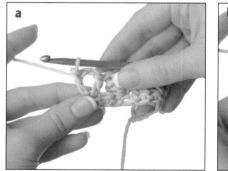

The Pattern

Row 1: SC into second CH from hook. SC into each CH across. CH 1 and turn.

Row 2: *1 popcorn V-st into second st, skip 2 sts, and 1 V-st into next st. Repeat from * to last 3 sts. Skip 2 sts and DC into last st. CH 3 and turn.

Row 3: *1 popcorn V-st into CH 2 space, and 1 V-st into next CH 2 space. Repeat from * to end of row. 1 DC into space between turning CH and DC of previous row. CH 3 and turn.

Row 4: *1 V-st into CH 2 space; work 1 popcorn V-st into next CH 2 space. Repeat from * to end of row. 1 DC into space between turning CH and DC of previous row. CH 3 and turn.

Repeat rows 3 and 4.

The Pattern in Plain English

The foundation chain for this pattern consists of a multiple of 8 plus 2, plus 1 for the turning chain (for example, 24 + 2 + 1 = 27).

  Row 1: Work 1 single crochet into the second chain from the hook. Continue to work 1 single crochet into each chain across the row. Chain 3 and turn.

2 **Row 2:** Starting in the second stitch of the row, *work 1 popcorn V-stitch, skip 2 stitches, and work 1 V-stitch. Repeat from the * across the row until 3 stitches remain. Skip 2 stitches and work 1 double crochet into the last stitch. Chain 3 and turn.

3 **Row 3:** Starting in the first chain 2 space, *work 1 popcorn V-stitch into the chain 2 space, and work 1 V-stitch into the next chain 2 space.

4 Repeat from the *, working into each chain 2 space across. Work 1 double crochet into the space between the turning chain and double crochet from the previous row. Chain 3 and turn.

5 **Row 4:** Starting with the first chain 2 space, *work 1 V-stitch into the chain 2 space, and work 1 popcorn V-stitch into the next chain 2 space. Repeat from the *, working into each chain 2 space across. Work 1 double crochet into the space between the turning chain and double crochet of the previous row. Chain 3 and turn.

6 Repeat rows 3 and 4.

chapter 10

Motifs and Fun Shapes

The fun and fast-to-crochet motifs presented here are a great way to practice reading patterns, and the finished products make great embellishments for scarves, hats, and other items. Work through some simple patterns in this chapter before you move on to the more complex patterns in Chapters 13 and 14.

Loopy Chain Flower

This quick and funky flower is made using loops of chain stitches worked into a round of single crochet.

Specifications

MATERIALS

The example in this tutorial was made with DK weight yarn and a 4.5 mm hook. You can use any yarn to make your own loopy chain flowers; choose a hook size appropriate for the yarn you've chosen.

TECHNIQUES USED

CH	Chain stitch
sl st	Slip stitch
SC	Single crochet

Note: See Chapter 3 for more on how to make these stitches.

Loopy Chain Flower Pattern

1 CH 2. Work 4 SC in the second chain from the hook (see photo). Join with a sl st. Gently pull the tail to tighten the ring.

This round of SC creates a base for the petals. Each petal is made with a loop of chain stitches worked into a SC from this round.

Note: See Chapter 4 for more on working in the round.

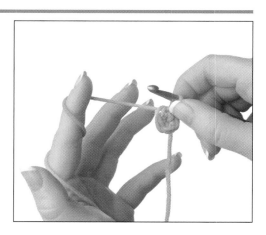

2 CH 8. Sl st into the first SC.

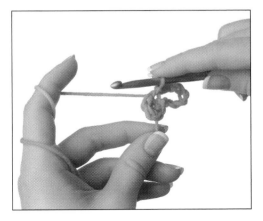

3 *CH 8. Sl st into the next SC, CH 8, and then sl st into the same SC.

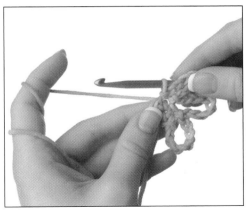

4 Repeat from * to create a total of 8 loopy petals. Sl st to join at the base of the first petal.

Simple Daisy

Easy to crochet, this simple daisy makes a sweet addition to any project. Use it as an appliqué, make it into a pin, or even use it to patch up a pair of old jeans.

Specifications

MATERIALS

The example in this tutorial was made with DK weight yarn and a 4.5 mm hook. You can use any yarn to make your own simple daisies; choose a hook size appropriate for the yarn you've chosen.

STITCHES USED

CH	Chain stitch
sl st	Slip stitch
SC	Single crochet
DC	Double crochet

Note: See Chapter 3 for more on how to make these stitches. See Chapter 4 for more on how to work in the round.

Simple Daisy Pattern

FOUNDATION ROUND

1. CH 2. Work 5 SC into the second CH from the hook. Join with a sl st. Gently pull on the tail to tighten the ring.

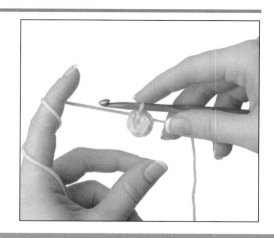

PETAL ROUND

Each petal is made by using a combination of stitches worked into 1 SC.

1 Starting in the first SC from the previous round, [CH 2, 3 DC, CH 2, sl st].

1 petal made.

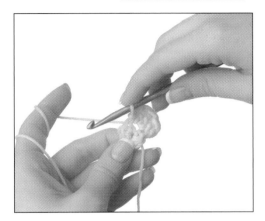

2 *Sl st into the next SC (a). Work 1 petal [CH 2, 3 DC, CH 2, sl st] into this SC (b).

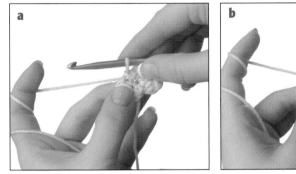

3 Repeat from * to create a total of 5 petals. Sl st to join at the base of the first petal.

4 Fasten off and weave in the ends.

Note: Instead of weaving in the yarn tails, use them to sew the daisy onto a crocheted project or tie it onto a pin.

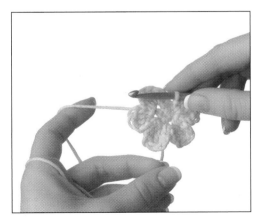

Add Layers to the Simple Daisy

It's easy to add another layer of petals to the simple daisy. Work one layer into the front loop and one into the back loop of the same round to create a three-dimensional flower.

Specifications

MATERIALS

The example in this tutorial was made with DK weight yarn and a 4.5 mm hook. You can use any yarn to make your own layered daisies; choose a hook size appropriate for the yarn you've chosen.

TECHNIQUES USED

CH   Chain stitch

sl st   Slip stitch

SC   Single crochet

DC   Double crochet

Working in front loop and back loop

Note: *See Chapters 3 and 6 for more on how to work these stitches.*

Simple Daisy Layers

FOUNDATION ROUND

❶ CH 2. Work 5 SC into the second CH from the hook. Join with a sl st into the first SC.

❷ Gently pull on the tail to tighten the ring.

PETAL ROUND 1

① Starting with the first SC from the foundation round, work 1 petal [CH 2, 3 DC, CH 2, sl st] into the front loop only (a).

② *Sl st into the next SC. Work 1 petal [CH 2, 3 DC, CH 2, sl st] into the front loop of this SC.

③ Repeat from * to create a petal in the front loop of each SC from the foundation round. Join with a sl st at the base of the first petal of the round (b).

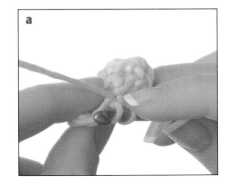

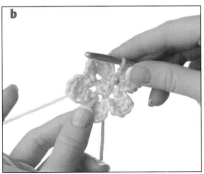

PETAL ROUND 2

① Sl st into the back loop of the first SC from the foundation round.

② Work the first petal [CH 2, 3 DC, CH 2, sl st] into the back loop of this SC.

③ *Sl st into the back loop of the next SC. Work 1 petal [CH 2, 3 DC, CH 2, sl st] into the back loop of this SC.

④ Repeat from * to create a petal in the back loop of each SC from the foundation round (see photo).

⑤ Join with a sl st at the base of the first petal of the round. Fasten off.

This leaf motif starts at the stem and builds out to create a lovely tapered leaf.

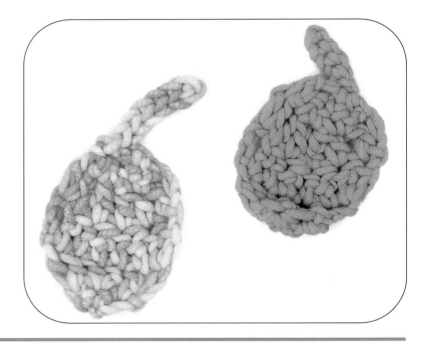

MATERIALS

The example in this tutorial was made with DK weight yarn and a 4.5 mm hook.

Any yarn can be used; choose a hook size appropriate for the yarn you've chosen.

TECHNIQUES USED

CH	Chain stitch
sl st	Slip stitch
SC	Single crochet
DC	Double crochet
DC TOG	Double crochet together

Note: *See Chapters 3 and 4 for more on how to make these stitches.*

Leaf Pattern

1. CH 2.
2. Row 1: Work 3 SC into the second CH from the hook. CH 3 and turn.
3. Row 2: Work 1 DC into the first st, work 2 DC into each of the next 2 sts. CH 3 and turn.

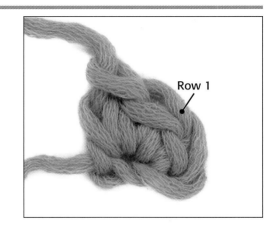

Row 1

④ **Row 3:** Work 1 DC into the first st, work 2 DC TOG over the next 2 sts, 2 DC TOG over the next 2 sts, and 2 DC into the last st. CH 1 and turn.

⑤ **Row 4:** Repeat row 3.

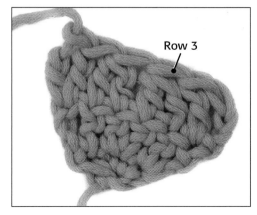

Row 3

⑥ **Row 5:** Work 2 SC TOG over the first 2 sts. Work 1 SC into each of the next 2 sts. Work 2 SC TOG over the last 2 sts.

⑦ Remove the hook from the loop. Insert the hook through the first st of the row, pick up the loop from the end of the row, and pull through.

⑧ CH 7 and work 1 sl st into each chain. Sl st to the body of the leaf. Fasten off.

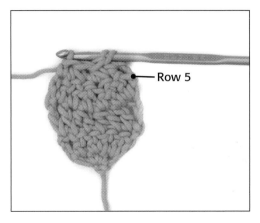

Row 5

Corkscrew

Increasing by too many stitches in each row creates a ruffle. Increasing by *far* too many stitches causes the work to turn in on itself, resulting in a corkscrew that makes a playful fringe or ornament.

Specifications

MATERIALS

The example in this tutorial was made with DK weight yarn and a 4.5 mm hook. You can use any yarn to make your own corkscrews; choose a hook size appropriate for the yarn you've chosen.

TECHNIQUES USED

CH	Chain stitch
sl st	Slip stitch
SC	Single crochet

Note: See Chapter 3 for more on how to make these stitches.

Corkscrew Pattern

1. CH any number—the longer the chain, the longer the corkscrew.
2. Sl st into the second CH from the hook. *Work 4 SC into the next CH (see photo under "Specifications" above).
3. Repeat from *, working into each CH across. Fasten off.

This simple motif works up quickly. The unusual shape adds interest to any project as an appliqué or as motifs that are joined.

Specifications

MATERIALS

The example in this tutorial was made with DK weight yarn and a 4.5 mm hook.

Any yarn can be used; choose a hook size appropriate for the yarn you've chosen.

TECHNIQUES USED

CH	Chain stitch
sl st	Slip stitch
SC	Single crochet
DC	Double crochet
TR	Treble crochet
DTR	Double treble

Note: *See Chapters 3 and 5 for more on how to make these stitches.*

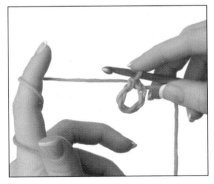

Teardrop Pattern

1. CH 6. Sl st to join the first chain to the last for working in the round. CH 1 (see photo under "Specifications" above).

2. Working into the center of the ring, make 3 SC, 1 DC, 3 TR, CH 1, 1 DTR, CH 1, 3 TR, 1 DC, 3 SC (see photo).

3. Sl st into the first SC at the beginning of the round to join. Fasten off (see top of page for completed teardrop).

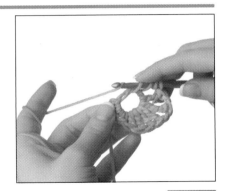

Bauble

This 3-D motif can be attached to any project. You can also think up any number of creative uses for it, like making a pet toy (insert a jingle bell in it) or a potpourri sachet!

Specifications

MATERIALS

The example in this tutorial was made with DK weight yarn and a 4.5 mm hook.

Any yarn can be used; choose a hook size appropriate for the yarn you've chosen.

TECHNIQUES USED

CH   Chain stitch

sl st   Slip stitch

SC   Single crochet

DC   Double crochet

Note: *See Chapter 3 for more on how to make these stitches.*

Bauble Pattern

This pattern is worked in the round. Do not turn your work at the end of a round.

1 CH 8. Sl st into the first CH to join for working in the round.

2 Round 1: CH 1. Work 1 SC into each chain around. Sl st into the first SC to join (8 SC total).

3 Round 2: CH 1. Work 2 SC into the first st and into each st from the previous round. Sl st to join (16 SC total).

4 Round 3: CH 2. Work 2 DC into the first st; work 1 DC into the next st. Work *2 DC into the next st and 1 DC into the next st. Repeat from * across the round (24 DC total). Sl st to the top of the first DC to join (see photo).

5 Round 4: CH 1. Work 1 SC into each st from the previous round. Sl st to join (24 SC total).

6 Round 5: CH 1. Work 1 SC into the first st, 2 SC TOG over the next 2 sts. Work *1 SC into the next st, 2 SC TOG over the next 2 sts. Repeat from * across the round. Sl st to join (16 SC total).

7 Round 6: CH 1. Work 2 SC TOG over the first 2 sts. *Work 2 SC TOG over the next 2 sts. Repeat from * around. Sl st to join (8 SC total) (see photo).

FINISH THE BAUBLE

8 Leaving a long tail, tie off. Lace the tail through the stitches of round 6 (see photo); pull to tighten and weave in the ends. Lace the other tail through the stitches of the foundation chain; pull to tighten. You might choose to use this tail to attach the bauble to a project.

Note: See Chapter 4 for more on basic finishing techniques.

9 Attach fringe to the stitches in the final round (see photo).

Note: See Chapter 12 for more on attaching fringe.

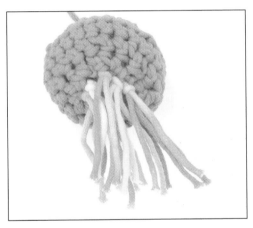

TIP

For added flair, stuff the bauble with a jingle bell or potpourri.

Triangles Using Increases or Decreases

Use simple shaping techniques to create a triangle shape. Start with a point and increase as you go, or start with a long row and decrease to a point.

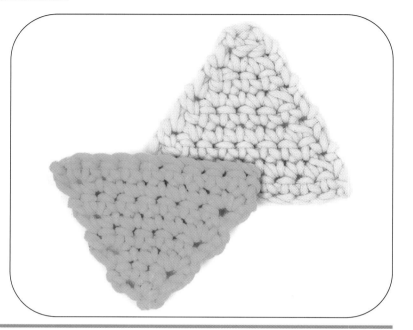

Specifications

MATERIALS

The example in this tutorial was made with DK weight yarn and a 4.5 mm hook.

Any yarn can be used; choose a hook size appropriate for the yarn you've chosen.

TECHNIQUES USED

CH	Chain stitch
sl st	Slip stitch
SC	Single crochet
SC TOG	Single crochet together

Note: *See Chapter 3 for more on how to make these stitches. Also, see Chapter 4 for more on increasing and decreasing.*

Decrease Triangle

1. CH any number plus 1 for the turning CH.

2. **Row 1:** Work 1 SC into the second loop from the hook. Work 1 SC into each CH across. CH 1 and turn.

3. **Row 2:** Work 2 SC TOG over the next 2 sts from the previous row. Work 1 SC into each st across to finish the row. CH 1 and turn.

4. Repeat row 2 to decrease 1 st per row until only 3 sts are left.

5. **Final row:** SC 3 TOG to complete the triangle. Fasten off.

Increase Triangle

1 CH 2.

2 Row 1: Work 3 SC into the second CH from the hook. CH 1 and turn.

3 Row 2: Work 2 SC into the first st of the previous row. Work 1 SC in each st across to finish the row. CH 1 and turn.

4 Repeat row 2 until the triangle is the desired size.

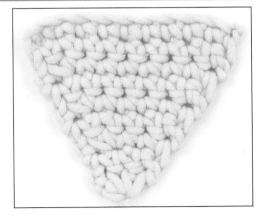

TIP

Appliqué triangles to completed projects for a playful look, especially for children's items. Consider making a large triangle to use as a head scarf, dish rag, or face cloth.

Triangle in the Round

Instead of making a triangle by increasing from a point or decreasing to a point (see previous section), you can easily work one up by crocheting in the round.

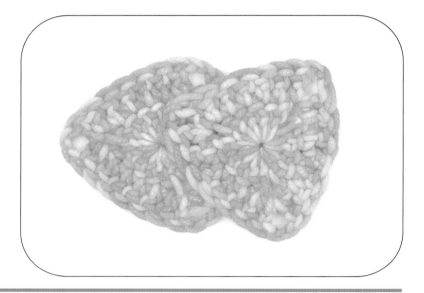

Specifications

MATERIALS

The example in this tutorial was made with DK weight yarn and a 4.5 mm hook.

Any yarn can be used; choose a hook size appropriate for the yarn you've chosen.

TECHNIQUES USED

CH   Chain stitch

sl st   Slip stitch

DC   Double crochet

Note: *See Chapter 3 for more on how to make these stitches. Also, see the section "Create a Ring Using a Loop" in Chapter 4.*

Triangle-in-the-Round Pattern

① Round 1: Using a loop to form a ring, CH 3 and work 4 DC into the ring. *CH 2, work 5 DC. Repeat from * once to complete the round. CH 2, sl st in the third CH of the CH 3 at the beginning of the round to join. Pull on the tail of the loop to tighten the center.

② Round 2: CH 3; this chain counts as 1 DC. Skip the first DC from the previous round. *Work 1 DC into each DC from the previous round until you reach the first CH space. Work [1 DC, CH 2, 1 DC] into the CH space. Repeat from * twice to complete the round. Sl st in the third CH of the CH 3 at the beginning of the round.

③ Repeat round 2 until the triangle is the desired size.

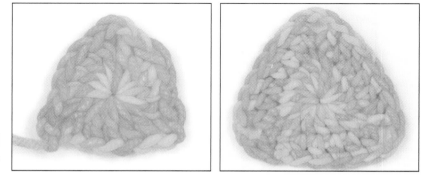

Pentagon

Pentagons are perfect for piecing together into scarves or afghans. They're just as simple to crochet as circles but add a bit of variety.

Specifications

MATERIALS

The example in this tutorial was made with DK weight yarn and a 4.5 mm hook.

Any yarn can be used; choose a hook size appropriate for the yarn you've chosen.

TECHNIQUES USED

CH   Chain stitch

sl st   Slip stitch

DC   Double crochet

Note: See Chapter 3 for more on how to make these stitches. Also, see the section "Create a Ring Using a Loop" in Chapter 4.

Pentagon Pattern

1. Round 1: Using a loop form ring, CH 3 and work 2 DC into the ring. *CH 2, work 3 DC into the ring. Repeat from * 4 times. CH 2, sl st in the third CH of the CH 3 at the beginning of the round to join. Pull on the tail of the loop to tighten the center (a).

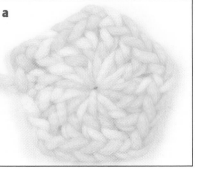

2. Round 2: CH 3; this chain counts as 1 DC. Skip the first DC from the previous round. Work 1 DC into each DC from the previous round until you reach the first CH space. Work [1 DC, CH 2, 1 DC] into the CH space. *Work 1 DC into each DC; work [1 DC, CH 2, 1 DC] into the CH space. Repeat from * 4 times to complete the round. Sl st in the third CH of the CH 3 at the beginning of the round.

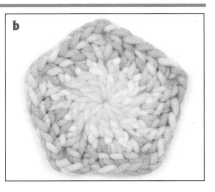

3. Repeat round 2 until the pentagon is the desired size (b). Fasten off.

Rectangle in the Round

This motif is worked in the round instead of in rows to create an interesting fabric of concentric rectangles.

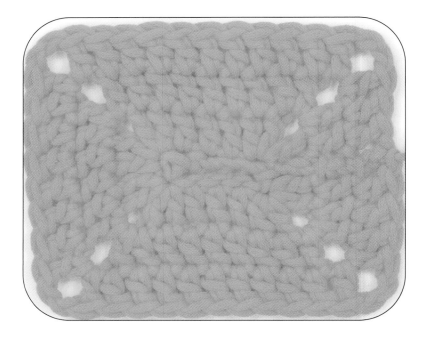

Specifications

MATERIALS

The example in this tutorial was made with DK weight yarn and a 4.5 mm hook.

Any yarn can be used; choose a hook size appropriate for the yarn you've chosen.

TECHNIQUES USED

CH   Chain stitch

sl st   Slip stitch

DC   Double crochet

Note: *See Chapter 3 for more on how to make these stitches.*

Rectangle Pattern

1 CH 6.

2 Round 1: Working into the top loop of the CH braid, work a sl st very loosely into the second CH from the hook and into every CH until the last CH. Work 2 sl st in the last CH to round the corner, and rotate the chain clockwise. Continue to work into the bottom loop of the CH, working 1 sl st into both remaining loops of each CH across the backside.

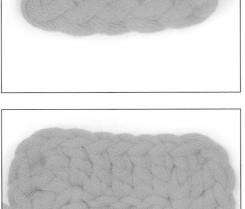

3 Round 2: CH 3; this chain counts as a DC. Work 1 DC into the first st of the round, CH 1, 2 DC into the next st. Work 1 DC into each of the next 3 sts. Work [2 DC in the next st, CH 1, 2 DC in the next] to create a corner.

4 Work [2 DC in the next st, CH 1, 2 DC in the next st] to create another corner. Work 1 DC into each of the next 3 sts. Work [2 DC in the next st, CH 1, 2 DC in the next st] to create another corner. Sl st to the third CH of the CH 3 from the beginning of the round.

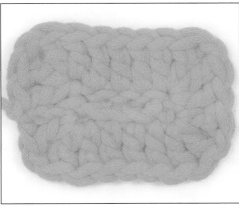

5 Round 3: CH 3; this chain counts as 1 DC. Skip the first DC from the previous round. *Work 1 DC into each DC from the previous round until the CH space; work [1 DC, CH 2, 1 DC] into the CH space (see photo).

6 Repeat from * 3 times. Work 1 DC into each DC from the previous round. Sl st in the third CH of the CH 3 at the beginning of the round.

7 Repeat round 3 until the rectangle is the desired size.

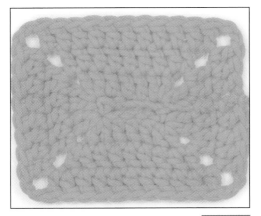

Granny Square

The traditional granny square has survived the decades because it's fun to make and easy to modify to suit your preferences. Granny squares make excellent building blocks for pieces like the purse on page 246 and for afghans.

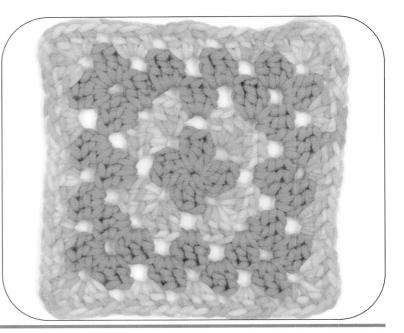

Specifications

MATERIALS

The example in this tutorial was made with DK weight yarn and a 4.5 mm hook.

Any yarn can be used; choose a hook size appropriate for the yarn you've chosen.

TECHNIQUES USED

CH	Chain stitch
sl st	Slip stitch
DC	Double crochet

Granny cluster: 3 DC in CH 1 space

Corner set: [CH 2, 3 DC, CH 2, 3 DC] in CH 2 space

Note: *See Chapter 3 for more on how to make these stitches. Also, see the section "Create a Ring Using a Loop" in Chapter 4.*

Granny Square Pattern

1 Round 1: Using a loop for a ring, CH 3 and work 2 DC into the ring. *CH 2, 3 DC into the ring. Repeat from * twice to create 2 more granny clusters. Sl st in the third CH of the CH 3 at the beginning of the round. Fasten off.

2 Round 2: Join the yarn in the next CH 2 space. Work [CH 3, 2 DC, CH 2, 3 DC] into the CH space. *CH 1. In the next CH space, work a corner set [CH 2, 3 DC, CH 2, 3 DC]. Repeat from * to work a corner set into each CH 2 space. Sl st in the third CH of the CH 3 at the beginning of the round. Fasten off.

Note: See Chapter 4 for information on how to join yarn.

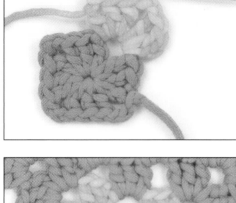

3 Round 3: Join the yarn in the next corner CH space. Work [CH 3, 2 DC, CH 2, 3 DC] into the CH space.

4 *CH 1. Work 1 granny cluster in each CH 1 space; CH 1. In the next CH 2 space, work a corner set [CH 2, 3 DC, CH 2, 3 DC].

5 Repeat from * to work into each CH space. Sl st in the third CH of the CH 3 at the beginning of the round. Fasten off.

Note: From here, the number of granny clusters worked into CH spaces between corner sets increases with each round.

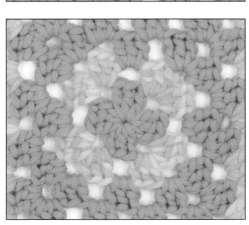

Mitered Square

A mitered square is created when you make a 90-degree bend by decreasing in the middle of each row. This is a fun way to make a square with an interesting look.

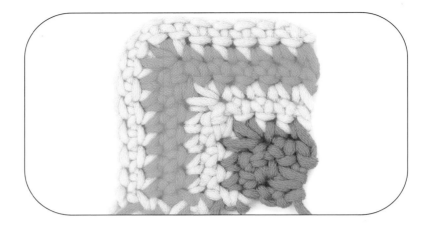

Specifications

MATERIALS

The example in this tutorial was made with weight yarn and a 4.5 mm hook.

You can use any yarn to make your own mitered squares; choose a hook size appropriate for the yarn you've chosen.

Stitch marker.

TECHNIQUES USED

CH   Chain stitch

sl st   Slip stitch

SC   Single crochet

Note: *See Chapter 3 for more on how to make these stitches.*

Mitered Square Pattern

Create a foundation chain that is an odd number, plus 1 for the turning chain.

1 Row 1: Work 1 SC in the second CH and each CH across. CH 1 and turn. Place a marker in the st at the center of the row.

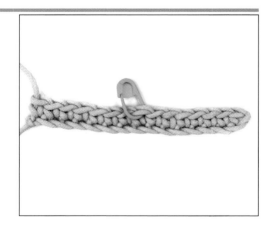

2 Row 2: Work 1 SC in each st across to the st before the marker. Remove the marker. Work 3 SC TOG over the center 3 sts. Work 1 SC into each st across to the end of the row, CH 1, and turn. Place the marker in the st at the center of the row.

3 Repeat row 2 until 3 sts are left in the row.

4 Final row: Work 3 SC TOG (see photo). Fasten off and weave in ends.

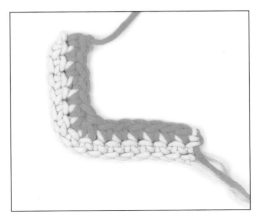

 TIP

This pattern looks great with stripes of color. You can join mitered squares together to make interesting patterns.

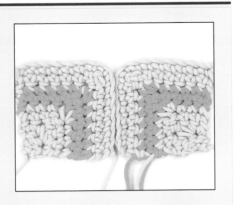

More Techniques

Working in multiple colors, making lace with a "broomstick," making knit-like stitches with Tunisian crochet, and crocheting with beads are just a few of the fascinating variations on crochet that can add an enormous amount of interest to your work.

Use Stripes to Add Color

Changing yarn color between rows is an easy way to give your fabric a variety of personalities, even if you're just working a simple stitch. Using the technique introduced in Chapter 4 on how to add a new ball of yarn to change color, you can easily crochet an infinite variety of striped patterns.

You can choose several colors and work each row in a different color.

Changing yarn color after several rows creates wider stripes.

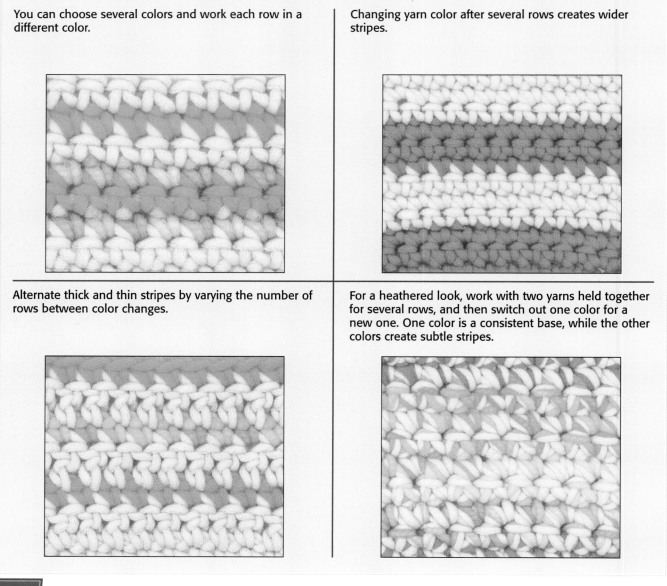

Alternate thick and thin stripes by varying the number of rows between color changes.

For a heathered look, work with two yarns held together for several rows, and then switch out one color for a new one. One color is a consistent base, while the other colors create subtle stripes.

Working with color designs is exciting. The simplest stitches can come to life just by changing color in prescribed spots to create a design. Follow a charted design to produce a stunning piece of work.

RIGHT SIDE AND WRONG SIDE

When the spaces between color changes are small, both colors can be carried across the row, working one color and carrying the other loosely across the wrong side of the piece. This kind of color work creates a *right side* (the side that shows in the picture; see a) and a *wrong side* (the side where the strands are hidden; see b). The stranded yarn is always carried on the wrong side. Be careful of this as you turn your work with each row.

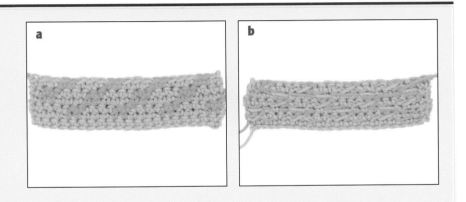

SECURE THE STRANDED YARN

To secure the stranded yarn, catch the stranded yarn every few stitches. To do so, allow the stranded yarn to be looped over by the stitch being worked (see photo).

If you catch the yarn securely enough, you can snip the strands and weave them in later to allow for better drape in your fabric.

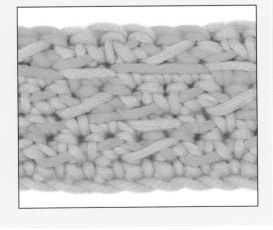

CONTINUED ON NEXT PAGE

FOLLOW THIS CHARTED PATTERN

Each square in the chart represents one stitch. For this pattern, you use only single crochet. (See Chapter 3 for more on single crochet.)

1. Start with a foundation chain that is a multiple of 20.

2. Begin working from the bottom-right corner of the chart and work 1 SC for each block.

3. Read the odd rows from right to left.

4. Read the even rows from left to right.

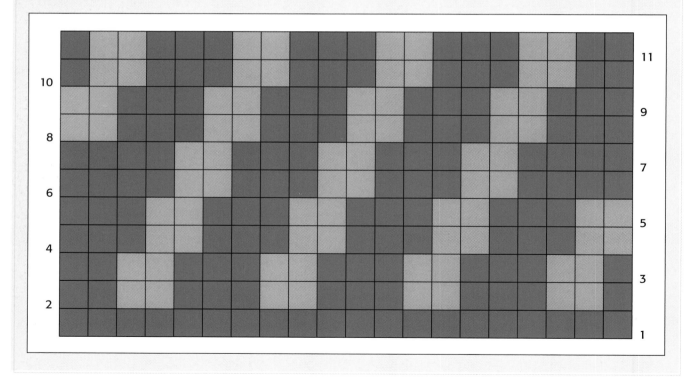

Intarsia is used for color patterns when the spaces between color changes are too large for stranding to be practical or when more than two yarns are in use. Instead of stranding the unused yarn across the work, you simply drop it and let it hang until you need it again.

Dropping one color and picking up another is simple. Using the old color, work the last stitch to the final step. Pick up the new color, and yarn over with both yarns held together to complete the stitch. Drop the old yarn, and continue with the new yarn.

Here is the front side of an intarsia swatch.

There is little difference between the front (a) and back (b) sides when a color pattern is worked with intarsia.

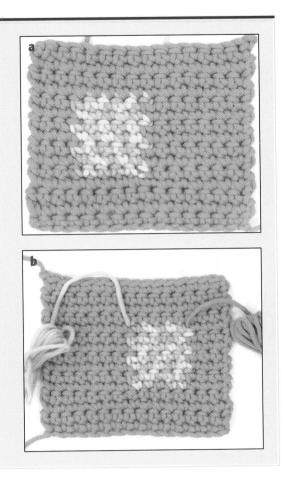

Photo b shows the unworked yarn dangling from the back of the intarsia swatch.

Many patterns list the precise amount of each color required; this is so you can make small balls or bobbins of each color. Keeping the colors tidy prevents confusion and tangles as you work.

CONTINUED ON NEXT PAGE

Follow This Charted Pattern Using Intarsia

Each square in the chart represents one stitch. For this pattern you use only single crochet. (See Chapter 3 for more on single crochet.)

1 Start with a foundation chain of 15.

2 Begin working from the bottom-right corner of the chart.

3 Read the odd rows from right to left.

4 Read the even rows from left to right.

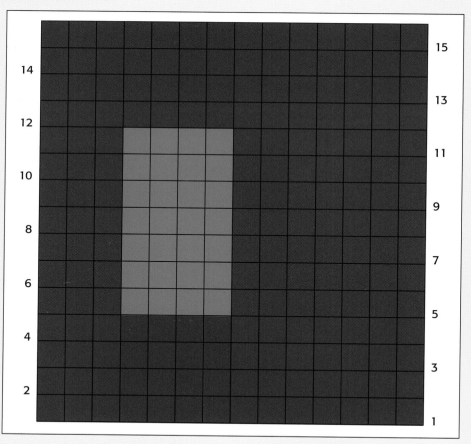

You make broomstick loops by slipping long loops onto any rod that has a wider diameter than the hook you're using. An actual broomstick is not necessary; large knitting needles work well for this stitch. The larger the "broomstick," the larger the loops.

Broomstick Loops

You can work these loops into any stitch. Start with a chain or row of any length.

Right-handed: Work from left to right, with the broomstick in your left hand.

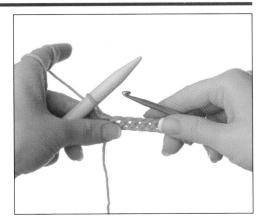

Left-handed: Work from right to left, with the broomstick in your right hand.

CONTINUED ON NEXT PAGE

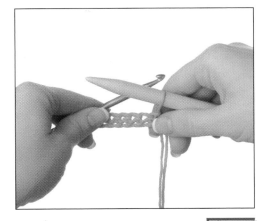

① Row 1: Insert the hook into the next stitch from the previous row, yarn over and draw the yarn through, lengthening this loop so that it can be placed on the broomstick (a). Leave the loop on the broomstick. Repeat across the row (b).

Note: *At the end of a row of broomstick loops, the loops are still on the broomstick. The next row locks these loops in place so they don't unravel.*

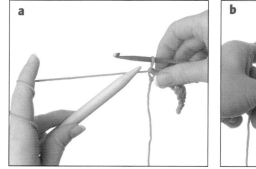
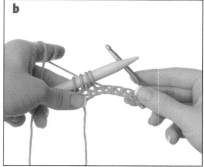

② Row 2: Slip 1 loop off the broomstick and onto the hook.

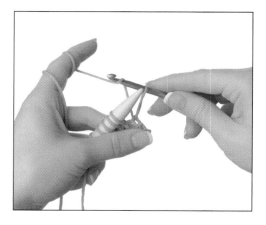

3 Yarn over and draw the yarn through both the loops on the hook. Chain 1.

4 Slip the next loop off the broomstick and onto the hook.

5 Yarn over and draw the yarn through both loops on the hook. Chain 1.

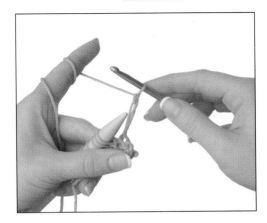

6 Repeat steps 4 and 5, working into every loop across the row.

7 Repeat rows 1 and 2.

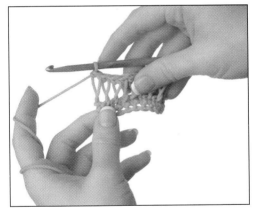

Make a Broomstick Loop Ruffle

Add this ruffle to any crocheted fabric for a loopy, ruffled edging.

Broomstick Loop Ruffle

Begin with a completed crocheted fabric.

1 **Row 1:** Work 2 single crochets into each stitch across. Chain 1 and turn.

2 **Row 2:** Work 1 broomstick loop into each single crochet across the row.

3 **Row 3:** *Slip 1 loop off the broomstick and onto the hook. Yarn over and draw the yarn through both loops on the hook. Chain 1. Repeat from the *, working into every loop across the row.

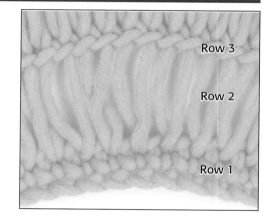

4 **Row 4:** *Work 1 broomstick loop into the top of the broomstick loop from the previous row.

5 Work 1 broomstick loop into the next chain stitch. Repeat from the *, working into each stitch across the row.

6 Repeat rows 3 and 4.

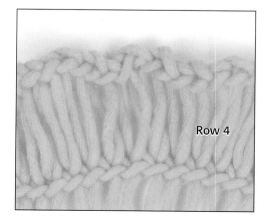

Broomstick loops are often worked together to create a traditional broomstick lace pattern such as this one.

Traditional Broomstick Lace

The foundation chain for this pattern consists of a multiple of 4 plus 1 for the turning chain.

1 Row 1: Work 1 broomstick loop into each chain across. (Refer to the section "Make Broomstick Loops.")

2 Row 2: *Slip 4 loops onto the hook, yarn over, and draw the yarn through all 4 loops to join them together. Chain 1. Work 4 single crochets into the center of the 4 loops you just joined.

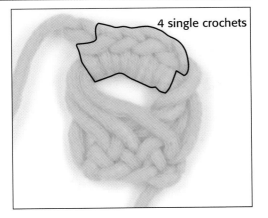

4 single crochets

3 Repeat from the * to complete the row.

4 Row 3: Work 1 broomstick loop into each single crochet from the previous round.

5 Repeat rows 2 and 3.

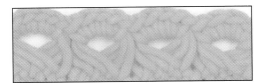

Make a Lover's Knot Trellis

Also known as a Solomon's knot, this stitch is made by drawing up a long loop and then locking it with a stitch at the top of the loop. Change the look of the stitch simply by changing the size of the loop! In this section, you will learn how to make a lover's knot and then how to make a trellis by using this stitch.

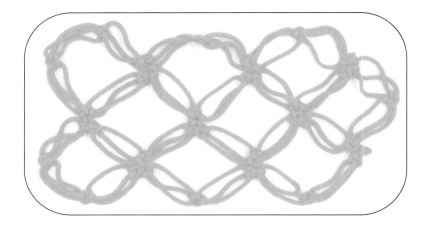

Lover's Knot Trellis

KNOT

1. Chain 1 and lengthen the loop on the hook (a).

   Note: *It is important that the length of each loop is the same so that the stitches match. A great way to keep track is to compare the loop to a given part of your finger. Knuckles make great guideposts for this. Here, the loop is being measured to the second knuckle of a finger (b).*

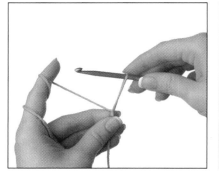
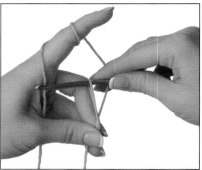

2. Yarn over and draw the yarn through the long loop (a).

3. Insert your hook between the long loop and the strand from the yarn over. Yarn over and draw the yarn through this space (b).

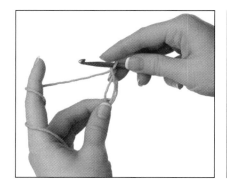
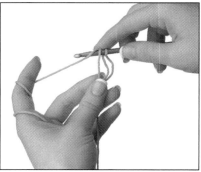

④ Yarn over and draw the yarn through both loops remaining on the hook.

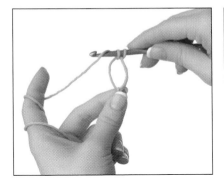
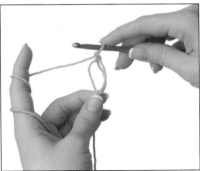

TRELLIS

The foundation row for this pattern consists of a multiple of 8 lover's knots.

① Row 1: Work 1 single crochet into the fifth lover's knot from the hook (a). *Work 2 lover's knots, skip 1 lover's knot from the previous row, and work 1 SC into the next lover's knot (b). Repeat from the * to complete the row. Work 3 lover's knots and turn.

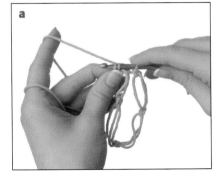
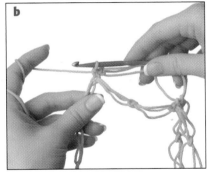

② Row 2: The previous row has created an arch with a lover's knot in the middle. Work 1 single crochet into the middle knot. *Work 2 lover's knots. Work 1 single crochet into the knot at the middle of the next arch (see photo). Repeat from the * to complete the row.

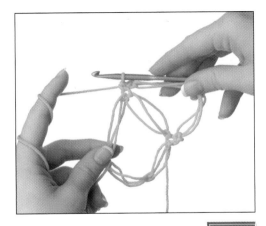

Make a Clones Knot Mesh

The Clones knot is fun to make once you get into the swing of it. First learn how to make a Clones knot, and then use it to add attitude to any simple mesh pattern.

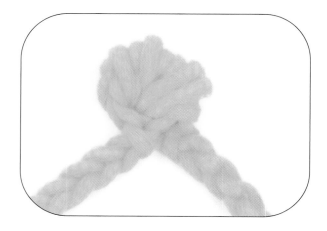

Clones Knot Mesh

KNOT

You work a Clones knot over the 3 chains closest to the hook.

1. Chain 3. Yarn over and wrap the yarn around the chain 3 as follows: Swing the hook from the front under the chain and to the back (a). Yarn over and swing back under the chain to the front (b).

2. Repeat step 1 four more times.

   There are now 11 loops on the hook.

   Note: As you work the yarn overs, you are working over and covering 3 chains. If you have covered more than that, simply push the loops together.

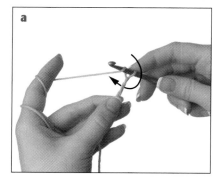

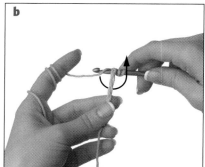

3. Yarn over and draw the yarn through all 11 loops (a).

4. Slip stitch into the third chain to complete the Clones knot (b).

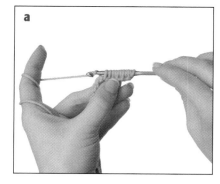

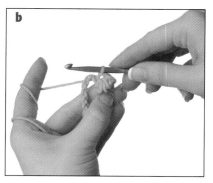

MESH

The foundation row consists of a multiple of 8 of the following combination:

*Work 1 Clones knot and chain 6.

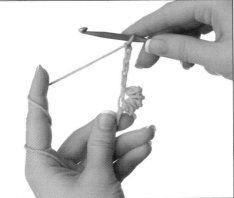

1. Row 1: Work 1 SC into the fourth Clones knot from the hook. *CH 6, work 1 Clones knot, and CH 6. Skip 1 Clones knot from the foundation row and work 1 SC into the next Clones knot. Repeat from the * to the end of the row.

2. Row 2: CH 6, work 1 Clones knot, CH 6, work 1 Clones knot, CH 6. Work 1 SC into the first Clones knot from the previous row. *CH 6, work 1 Clones knot. CH 6, work 1 SC into the next Clones knot from the previous row. Repeat from the * to finish the row.

3. Repeat row 2 to the desired length.

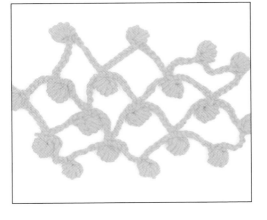

Tunisian Simple Stitch

It has been said that Tunisian crochet—also known as Afghan stitch—is like a cross between knitting and crocheting. You make each row in two steps by using a very long crochet hook: First, all the stitches are picked up, and then they are bound off. Tunisian crochet creates a fabric that is flat and has a unique texture. The pattern abbreviation is Tss.

Rows

FOUNDATION FORWARD ROW

1. Make a chain equal to the number of stitches you require.
2. Insert your hook into the second chain. Yarn over and draw the yarn through.

   There are now 2 loops on the hook (see photo).

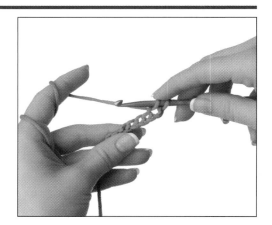

3. Insert the hook into the next chain and draw the yarn through.

   There are now 3 loops on the hook (a).
4. Repeat step 3 until you reach the end of the row. Do not turn your work.

   You now have 1 loop on your hook for each chain (b).

FOUNDATION RETURN ROW

Note: *You work the foundation return row with the right side of the work facing you. Do not turn the work.*

1 Yarn over and draw the yarn through 1 loop on the hook.

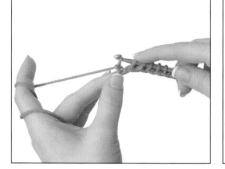 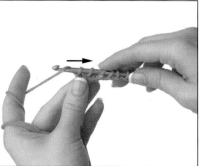

2 Yarn over and draw the yarn through 2 loops on the hook.

You are essentially binding off each stitch that you picked up in the forward row.

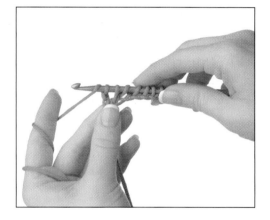

3 Repeat step 2 until you reach the end of the return row. At the last 2 stitches of the row, yarn over and draw through the final 2 stitches.

There is now 1 loop on the hook.

CONTINUED ON NEXT PAGE

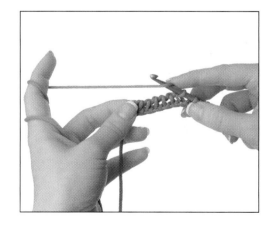

FORWARD ROW

1 Skip the first vertical bar from the previous row. Insert your hook behind the next vertical bar (a).

Note: *Each vertical bar corresponds to 1 Tunisian simple stitch.*

2 Yarn over and draw the yarn through.

There are now 2 loops on the hook (b).

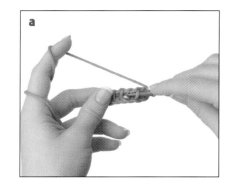
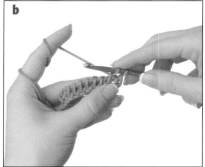

3 Insert the hook behind the next vertical bar (see photo). Yarn over and draw the yarn through.

4 Repeat step 3 until 1 stitch remains.

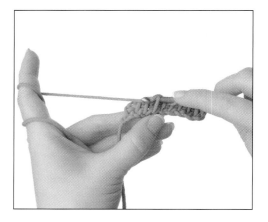

5 For the last stitch in the forward row, insert the hook into both vertical bars at the end of the row.

6 Yarn over and draw the yarn through.

You now have as many loops on your hook as there are stitches in the previous row.

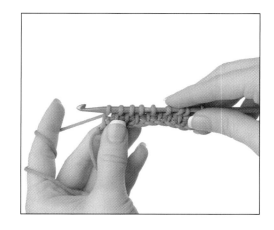

RETURN ROW

Note: *You work the Tunisian simple stitch return row with the right side of the work facing you. Do not turn the work.*

 Yarn over and draw the yarn through 1 loop on the hook.

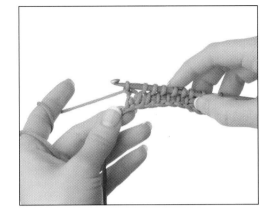

② Yarn over and draw the yarn through 2 loops on the hook.

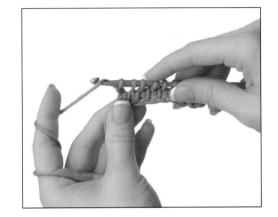

③ Repeat step 3 until you reach the end of the return row.

There is now 1 loop on the hook.

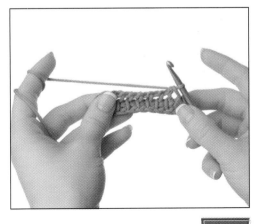

Tunisian Knit Stitch

The Tunisian knit stitch creates a fabric that looks much like the *right* side of knitted stockinette stitch. Its pattern abbreviation is Tks.

Rows

FORWARD ROW

1. Work a foundation row as you would for Tunisian simple stitch. (See the preceding section, "Tunisian Simple Stitch.")

2. Skip the first stitch from the previous row. Working between 2 vertical bars, insert your hook from front to back under both horizontal strands (a).

3. Yarn over and draw the yarn through.

   There are now 2 loops on the hook (b).

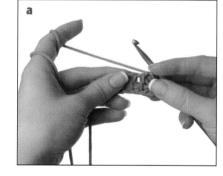
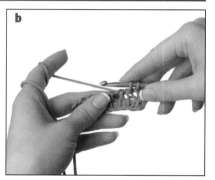

4. Insert the hook from front to back under the next pair of horizontal strands (a). Yarn over and draw the yarn through.

5. Repeat step 3 until you have completed the forward row (b).

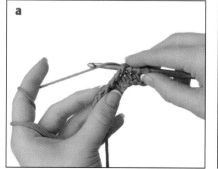

RETURN ROW

Note: *You work the Tunisian knit stitch return row with the right side of the work facing you. Do not turn the work.*

1 Yarn over and draw the yarn through 1 loop on the hook (see photo).

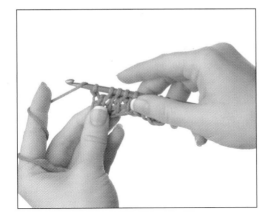

2 Yarn over and draw the yarn through 2 loops on the hook.

3 Repeat step 2 until you reach the end of the return row.

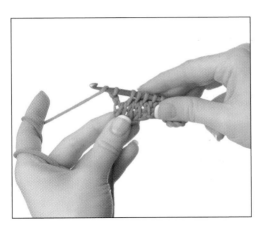

There is now 1 loop on the hook.

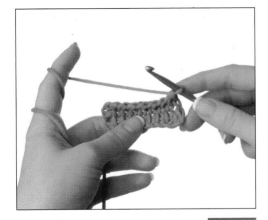

Tunisian Purl Stitch

The Tunisian purl stitch creates a fabric that looks much like the *wrong* side of knitted stockinette stitch. Its pattern abbreviation is Tps.

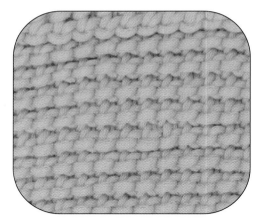

Rows

FOUNDATION FORWARD ROW

1. Make a chain equal to the number of stitches you require.

2. Holding the yarn in front of your work, insert the hook into the second chain (a). Yarn over and draw the yarn through (b).

   There are now 2 loops on the hook.

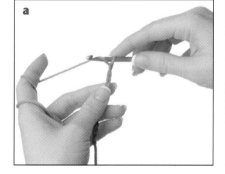
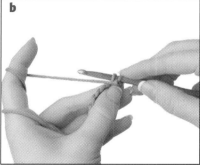

3. Holding the yarn in front of your work, insert the hook into the next chain and draw the yarn through.

   There are now 3 loops on the hook (a).

4. Repeat step 3 until you reach the end of the row. Do not turn your work.

   You now have 1 loop on your hook for each chain (b).

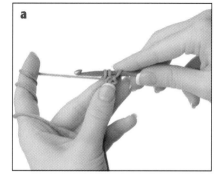

FOUNDATION RETURN ROW

Work the foundation return row as you would for Tunisian simple stitch. (See the earlier section "Tunisian Simple Stitch.")

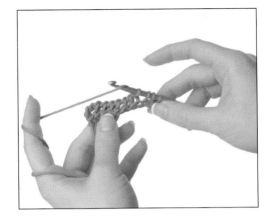

FORWARD ROW

1. Skip the first stitch from the previous row. Hold your hook with the yarn in front of the work (a) and insert it behind the next vertical bar, as you would if you were working Tunisian simple stitch.

2. Yarn over and draw the yarn through (b).

   There are now 2 loops on the hook.

3. Insert the hook behind next vertical bar. Yarn over and draw the yarn through. Repeat until 1 stitch remains.

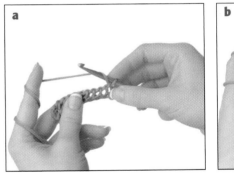

4. For the last stitch in the forward row, insert the hook into both vertical bars at the end of the row (a).

5. Yarn over and draw the yarn through (b).

6. Work the return row as you would for Tunisian simple stitch.

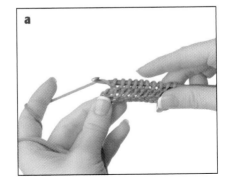

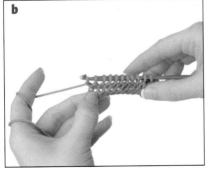

Increase in Tunisian Crochet

Learn how to shape your Tunisian crochet work. You can increase at the end of a forward or return row or between stitches in a forward row.

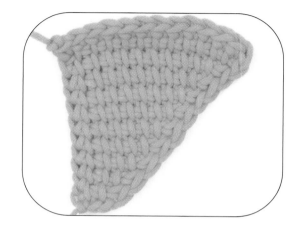

INCREASE WITHIN A FORWARD ROW

To increase within a forward row, pick up extra loops by working into both a horizontal and a vertical strand of the same stitch.

1. Insert your hook into the next horizontal strand. Yarn over and draw the yarn through (a).

2. Insert the hook into the next vertical bar. Yarn over and draw the yarn through (b).

   You have picked up 2 loops from the same stitch, resulting in an increase of 1 stitch.

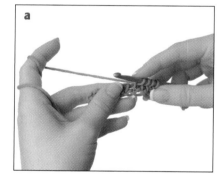

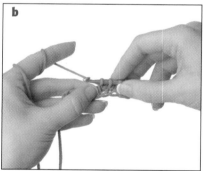

INCREASE AT THE END OF A FORWARD ROW

1. When you have reached the end of a forward row, loosely make 1 chain for each stitch you need to increase by, plus 1 (a).

2. Remove the hook from the last chain, drawing the loop long to hold your place (b).

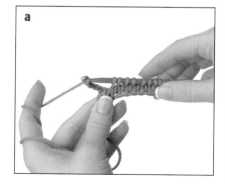

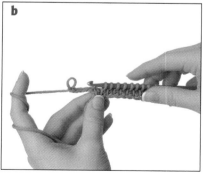

③ Insert the hook into the back loop of the first chain (a). Keep this loop on your hook.

④ Pick up the back loop of each remaining chain.

⑤ Return the last loop to your hook, pulling it tighter to fit snugly (b).

⑥ Work the return row as usual.

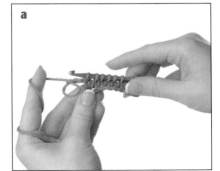

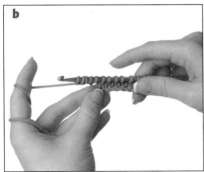

INCREASE AT THE END OF A RETURN ROW

① Work the return row to the end. One loop remains on the hook. Make 1 chain for each stitch you need to increase by (a).

② On the next forward row, skip the first chain. Insert the hook into the second chain, yarn over, and draw up a loop. Repeat for each chain (b).

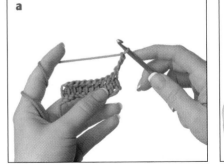

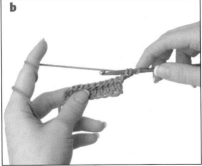

③ Pick up a loop in the first vertical bar. (You skip this bar on non-increase rows.) Continue to work a forward row as usual.

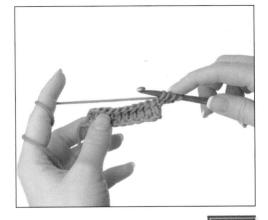

Decrease in Tunisian Crochet

Learn how to shape your Tunisian crochet work. You make decreases in the forward row by working two stitches together.

Decrease

1. Insert your hook behind the next 2 vertical bars.
2. Yarn over and draw the yarn through both bars.

   You now have only 1 loop to work in the return row, thus decreasing by 1 stitch.

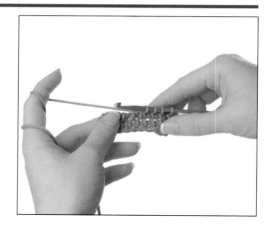

3. Work the return row as usual. (See the earlier section "Tunisian Simple Stitch.")

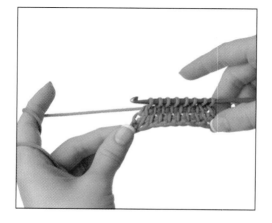

The final row of Tunisian crochet is
worked differently from the rest of the
piece. Stitches are bound off in the
forward row, resulting in a neat,
finished edge.

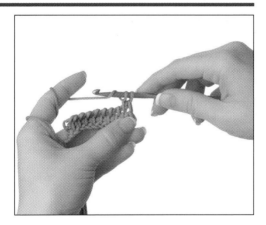

Bind Off

The final row of a Tunisian crochet piece is the *bind-off* row. You work only
a forward row, and you bind off stitches as you go.

1 At the beginning of a forward row, insert your hook behind the second vertical bar. Yarn over and draw the yarn through.

You now have 2 loops on your hook.

2 Yarn over and draw the yarn through both loops on the hook.

You now have 1 loop on your hook. You have bound off 1 stitch.

3 *Insert your hook behind the next vertical
bar. Yarn over and draw the yarn through.
Yarn over and draw the yarn through
both loops on the hook (a). Repeat from
the * until the end of the row.

You have 1 loop remaining on your hook.

4 Cut the yarn, leaving a 6-inch tail. Draw
the yarn through the loop to fasten off (b).

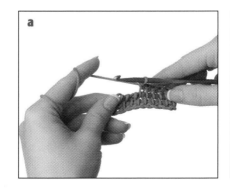

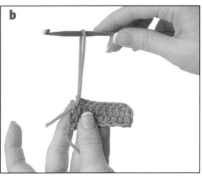

Free-form Crochet

Free-form is to crochet what jamming is to music. Combining the crochet skills you already have with a variety of stitches, colors, and yarns, you can create truly unique, stunning pieces of art.

Free-Form

TO START

Free-form crochet is made without a pattern or guidelines. Making free-form pieces is a great way to use up small amounts of yarn and leftovers from completed projects, and to play with new stitches and patterns as you learn. Just gather several yarns that complement each other and start crocheting!

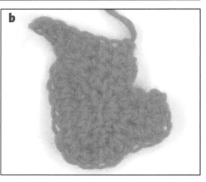

1 Use the stitch of your choice to create a shape of any sort. It can be a perfect circle (a), square, or rectangle, or it can be an amorphous blob (b).

ALTERNATIVE 1: MAKE SEVERAL PIECES

2 Make several more shapes out of different yarns.

3 Lay out the pieces and rearrange them until you like the way the configuration looks.

④ Attach the pieces together by using slip stitch or any stitch you prefer. (See Chapter 12 for more on joining pieces.)

ALTERNATIVE 2: JOIN YARN

① Use the stitch of your choice to create a shape of any sort. It can be a perfect circle, square, or rectangle, or it can be an amorphous blob.

② Instead of crocheting several separate pieces, you can build upon your initial piece by joining new yarns and crocheting shapes as you go. (See Chapter 4 for more on joining new yarn.)

 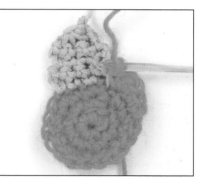

TIP

Use yarns from a similar color family to unite your work into a harmonious piece of art.

Chain a 12-inch cord and attach it in two places to your free-form creation. Use the cord to hang your piece on the wall.

You can make bags, hats, and garments out of free-form pieces. Experiment!

Filet Crochet

Filet crochet is a simple form of crochet that depicts shapes and pictures in thread. This style of crochet is popular for use in home décor as curtains, tablecloths, edgings, and more. Explore the potential of filet crochet to make modern and interesting pieces!

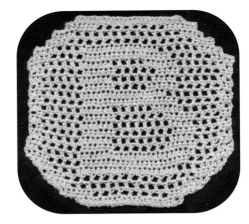

COLORS AND GRIDS

Filet crochet is traditionally made with cotton thread and a steel crochet hook. Traditionally only white thread was used, but it is certainly acceptable to experiment with colors. Designs are based on a grid. The grid usually consists of double crochet stitches and chains that combine to create a mesh of squares.

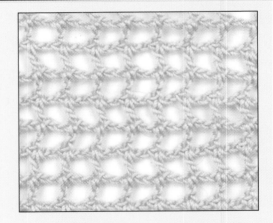

FILET CROCHET CHARTS

Filet crochet designs are depicted in charts, in which each box represents one square of the grid. (See Chapter 9 for more on charts.) Read the chart beginning from the bottom right. Odd-numbered rows are read from right to left; even-numbered rows are read from left to right.

An abundance of books and websites offer filet crochet charts.

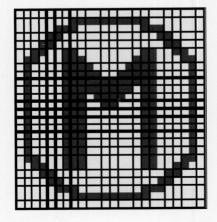

Make Filet Crochet

Filet crochet utilizes a grid base and positive and negative space to create shapes and pictures. Using a steel hook and cotton crochet thread, follow a chart to create delicate edgings and home décor pieces and garments.

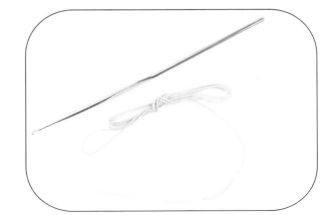

Filet Crochet

WORK AN OPEN BLOCK

An open block consists of [chain 2, 1 double crochet] over 3 stitches (or the foundation chain) from the previous row.

1 Where you want the block to begin (a), chain 2 (b). Skip 2 stitches. Work 1 double crochet into the next double crochet.

2 Repeat step 1 until a filled block is required.

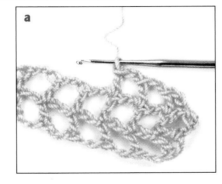

WORK A FILLED BLOCK

A filled block consists of 3 double crochets over 3 stitches (or the foundation chain) from the previous row.

If you're working into an open block from the previous row:

1 Work 2 double crochets into the next chain 2 space. Work 1 double crochet into the next double crochet.

2 Repeat step 1 until an open block is required.

If you're working into a filled block from the previous row:

1 Work 1 double crochet into each of the next 3 double crochets.

2 Repeat step 1 until an open block is required.

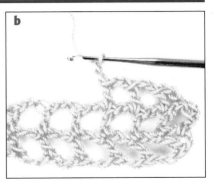

Open block

Filled block

Full a Crocheted Item

If you've ever accidentally tossed a wool sweater into the washing machine, you know that wool shrinks when agitated. Although you won't make that mistake again with a sweater, you may find that *fulling* pieces such as bags, slippers, and hats creates uniquely textured and durable products. (Note: This technique is frequently referred to as *felting*, although *fulling* is technically the correct term.)

How to Full

Sometimes erroneously referred to as *felting* (which pertains to the act of agitating unstitched fibers), *fulling* is the process of agitating 100% wool crocheted (or knitted) fabric in water. Fulling results in a fuzzy, dense fabric that is extremely strong and durable. Although wool blends full to varying extents, it is best to work with 100% wool that has not been treated to become machine washable (otherwise known as *superwash*).

① Crochet the project you intend to full. It is generally recommended to use a hook that is larger than recommended for your yarn. Be sure that your crocheted piece is larger than the fulled product should be in order to accommodate the shrinkage that results from fulling, and that your stitches are looser than normal.

② Place your crocheted piece into a mesh bag, zippered laundry bag, or pillowcase. Doing so will keep the piece from becoming stretched and distorted during agitation.

③ Set your washing machine to a warm or hot wash and add a small amount of mild soap or detergent. Place the mesh bag and one or two pairs of jeans into the machine. The jeans help with agitation.

Allow the agitation cycle to go for about 5 minutes, and then check on your crocheted piece. If it has not yet shrunk to the desired size, return it to the machine for more agitation. Continue to check it every 5 minutes until it is the desired size. You may have to run the machine through several agitation cycles.

⑤ When you have finished fulling your piece (see photo), rinse it gently, without wringing. You may run it through the spin cycle if you'd like, but it is not necessary, and it might warp a large item. If you choose not to spin, wrap the piece in a towel or two and press to remove any excess water.

⑥ Block your piece. (See Chapter 12.) If you are blocking a 3-D item such as a bag or a hat, fill the item with rolled towels or plastic bags until it is the proper shape. Let it dry.

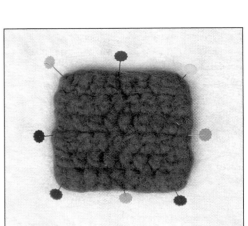

Crochet with Beads

Beads can add a playful or elegant element to crochet work. Experiment with beads of different sizes, shapes, and textures. Here are the basics you need to start your adventures with beads and crochet. You're bound to create some masterpieces along the way!

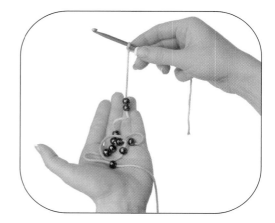

Using Beads

TO START

Patterns calling for bead crochet will specify the quantity and size of beads required. Thread all the beads you need onto the yarn before you begin to crochet.

1. Fold a piece of thread over the yarn tail.

   This folded piece of thread works as a flexible needle! Think of the ends of the thread as the point of a needle.

2. Slide beads onto the thread "needle" and then onto the yarn.

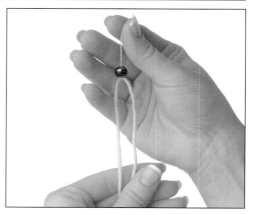

WORK BEADS INTO A CROCHET STITCH

1. Before completing the final step of any stitch, slide a bead close to your hook. (The example in the photo uses single crochet.)

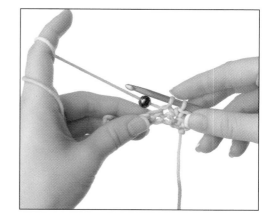

2 Yarn over and pull through to complete the stitch. This step secures a bead in the stitch. The bead sits on the side of the fabric facing away from you as you work the row.

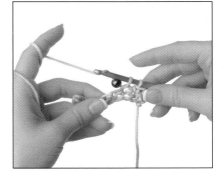

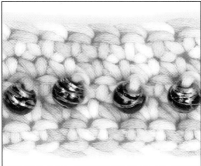

EXPERIMENT WITH OTHER STITCHES

Beads can be worked into any crochet stitch. Here is an example of working beads into a double crochet stitch.

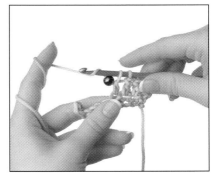

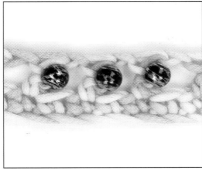

Slip a bead into the final step of a lover's knot. This might sound tricky, but it's the same as working simpler stitches. Give it a try!

chapter 12

Final Details and Finishing

You've completed crocheting a project. Congratulations! But chances are you're not done yet. This chapter covers the final steps to finishing a project and presents some basic embellishments to add as final touches.

Sometimes things go awry and you don't know why. Before you throw your crochet project across the room or rip it out entirely, take a look and figure out what went wrong. You'll learn from your mistakes and may be able to correct them easily.

Catch Common Mistakes

If your piece is getting narrower or wider where it's not supposed to, count the number of stitches in the row and compare that number against:

- The number of stitches the pattern says you should have in the row.
- The number of stitches in each of the past several rows. You might find that you accidentally increased or decreased all at once or over several rows.

The best way to prevent mistaken increases and decreases is to keep track of how many stitches you are working in each row. By doing so, you'll be able to catch mistakes before you've worked too far.

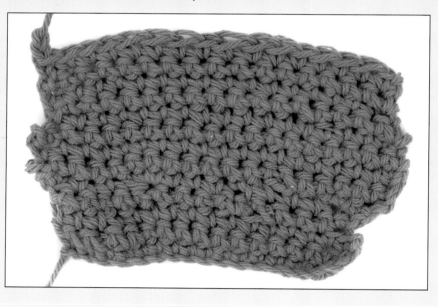

ACCIDENTALLY DECREASE?

Look for accidental decreases by

- Holding the piece up to a light or a window and looking for holes caused by skipped stitches.
- Examining your piece to see if you skipped any stitches mid-row (see photo).

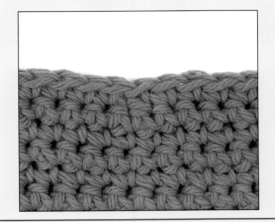

OMIT THE FINAL STITCH?

Did you accidentally omit the final stitch in the previous row? This is easy to do when you're making taller stitches because the turning chain that counts as a stitch can be easy to overlook.

ACCIDENTALLY INCREASE?

Look for accidental increases. Did you work more than one stitch into the same stitch when you weren't supposed to?

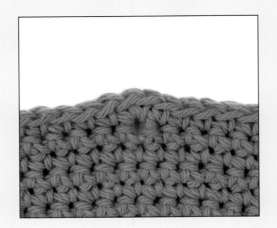

WORK IN THE TURNING CHAIN?

Did you accidentally work into a chain from the turning chain as if it was the first stitch of the row when you weren't supposed to?

Once you have identified a mistake, choose the best way to fix it. Remember that even experts make mistakes; don't be discouraged!

RIP BACK

In crochet, it's easy to rip back to a mistake. If you choose to rip back, simply tug gently on your working yarn to unravel the stitches to the error. Then pick up at that point in the pattern.

DO A SNEAKY FIX

Sometimes the mistake is as minimal as one decrease or increase, and it won't look terrible to simply compensate for it instead of ripping out the rows you worked so hard on. Fix by following these steps:

1. Diagnose the cause of the decrease or increase so that you don't repeat it.

2. Work an increase to correct an accidental decrease or a decrease to correct an accidental increase. Choose a place in the row where this correction will disappear as much as possible.

 TIP

Read through your pattern carefully, making notes to help you through tricky spots.

After all the time, energy, and love involved in making crocheted items, it's important to care for them properly so that they remain in excellent condition for as long as possible.

Maintain Your Crocheted Items

WASH CROCHETED ITEMS

All yarns are not created equal. Some are extremely delicate, and others are so durable you'd think they were made of steel.

When it comes to washing your crocheted items, be sure to follow the care instructions on the yarn label (see Chapter 2).

If you're giving an item as a gift, include a tag with care instructions and fiber information so the recipient knows how to wash the item correctly.

Made for you by Pam with lots of love!
This sweater is 100% wool.
Either dry clean it or hand wash it in warm water with a mild detergent.
Rinse it in warm water and lie out flat to dry.

STORE CROCHETED ITEMS

Store crocheted items in a clean, dry area away from pets. If the items are made of natural fibers, be sure to include cedar or lavender to repel moths and other pests that can wreak havoc.

Make a Buttonhole

Buttons are functional and decorative additions to crocheted garments and accessories. They come in all shapes, sizes, colors, and textures, and it's simple to incorporate them into your work. Here are two basic methods for making a buttonhole to fit any button.

Make a Buttonhole within a Row

Use this technique to make a horizontal buttonhole within a row of crochet.

1 Work up to the point where you will insert a buttonhole. Chain 3, skip 3 stitches (see photo), and continue in pattern to the end of the row. Make a turning chain and turn.

We used a 3-stitch buttonhole for this example. Depending on the size of your button, you may need to make your buttonhole larger or smaller. Simply compare the button to the buttonhole to make sure that they're a perfect fit. Adjust the number of skipped stitches and chains in order to get a good fit.

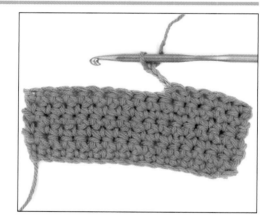

2 Work the next row according to the pattern, working 3 stitches as called for into the chain-3 space.

You've made a horizontal buttonhole.

chapter 12

Make a Buttonhole across Rows

Use this technique to make a vertical buttonhole over 2 or more rows of crochet.

1. Work to the point where you will insert
   a buttonhole (a). Make a turning chain
   and turn (b).

2. Work back to the beginning of your work.
   Make a turning chain and turn.

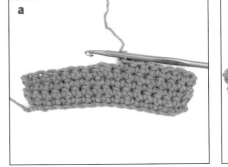
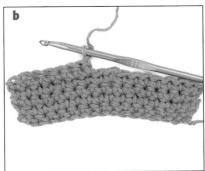

3. Work to the end of the short row and fasten off.

4. Join the yarn 1 stitch from the end of the first short row. *Work in pattern to
   the end of the short row. Make a turning chain and turn.

5. Repeat from * twice.

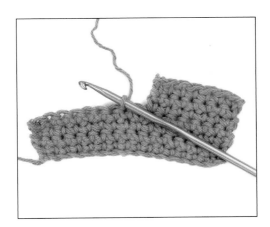

6. Work in pattern to the end of the short
   row. Chain 1 (a). Work the next stitch into
   the last stitch from step 3. Continue to
   the end of the row, work a turning chain,
   and turn.

   You've made a vertical buttonhole (b).

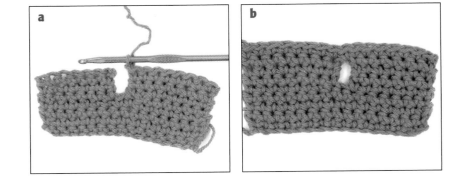

Seam Pieces Together by Sewing

Inevitably, some of the projects you crochet will need to be assembled in the end. Seaming might seem tedious, but the thrill of putting on a completed sweater for the first time can't be matched!

You can use one of several techniques to attach crocheted pieces together.

Create a Whipstitch Seam

A whipstitch seam is perhaps the easiest seam to sew, and it works best along straight edges.

1 Hold together the 2 pieces to be seamed, with their right sides together and with stitches or rows matched up.

> **Note:** The right side is the side that shows when the garment is worn. The wrong side is the side worn against the skin, or the side where the ends are woven in. When right sides are held facing each other for seaming, the piece will later be turned right side out, hiding the seam on the inside.

2 Using matching yarn or thread and a yarn needle, begin on the right by inserting the needle from back to front through the first stitch or row of each piece (a).

3 Bringing the needle over the top of the work, insert it from back to front through the next pair of stitches to the left (b).

Repeat step 3 to the end of the seam. Fasten off and weave in the tail.

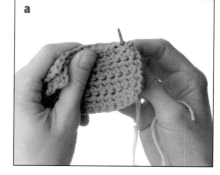

Create a Backstitch Seam

Backstitch creates a sturdy seam and is suited for use on curved or angled edges.

1. Hold together the 2 pieces to be seamed with their right sides together and with stitches or rows matched up. Using matching yarn or thread and a yarn needle, begin on the right by inserting the needle from front to back through the first stitch or row of each piece (a).

2. Insert the needle from back to front through the next pair of stitches to the left (b).

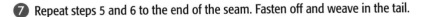

3. Insert the needle from front to back through the first pair of stitches again.

4. Skipping the next pair of stitches to the left, insert the needle from back to front through the next pair of stitches to the left.

5. Insert the needle from front to back into the pair of stitches to the right.

6. Skipping 1 pair of stitches, insert the needle from back to front into the next pair of stitches to the left.

7. Repeat steps 5 and 6 to the end of the seam. Fasten off and weave in the tail.

Seam Pieces Together by Crocheting

As an alternative to sewing pieces together, you can use slip stitch or single crochet to create a seam. These techniques are quick and create sturdy and optionally decorative seams.

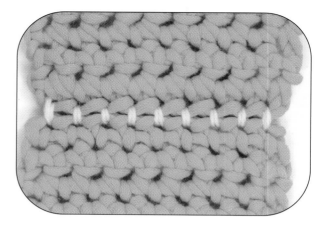

Create a Slip Stitch Seam

Slip stitching creates a simple seam and is suited for use on irregularly shaped edges.

1 Hold together the two pieces to be seamed with their right sides together and with stitches or rows matched up.

> *Note: The right side is the side that shows when the garment is worn. The wrong side is the side worn against the skin, or the side where your ends are woven in. When right sides are held facing each other for seaming, the piece will later be turned right side out, hiding the seam on the inside.*

2 Using matching yarn and an appropriately sized crochet hook, begin on the right by inserting the hook from front to back through both loops of each of the first pair of stitches, or through each of the first pair of rows.

> *Note: If your pieces are made from bulky yarn, you may choose to create your seam through only one loop of each stitch to keep the seam flat and neat.*

3 Yarn over and draw the yarn through both stitches and through the loop on the hook, creating 1 slip stitch.

Repeat steps 2 and 3 to the end of the seam, working into the next pair of stitches or rows to the left. Fasten off and weave in the tail.

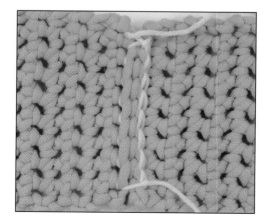

Create a Single Crochet Seam

Single crochet creates a bulky seam that is decorative if worked on the outside of a piece.

 Hold together the two pieces to be seamed with their right sides together and with stitches or rows matched up.

Alternatively, you can work this seam with the *wrong sides* together, to have the seam show on the right side.

2 Using matching yarn and an appropriately sized crochet hook, begin on the right by inserting the hook from front to back through both loops of each of the first pair of stitches, or through each of the first pair of rows.

3 Yarn over and draw the yarn through both stitches. Yarn over again and draw the yarn through both loops on the hook, creating 1 single crochet.

4 Repeat steps 2 and 3 to the end of the seam, working into the next pair of stitches or rows to the left. Tie off and weave in the tail.

Note: *Take care not to work your stitches too tightly. Staying loose keeps your seams flexible and maintains the drape of your garment.*

Make a Single Crochet Edging

Even the most basic item in a simple stitch can benefit from a neat or decorative edging. Crocheting around a finished piece not only makes edges look neat, but it can also provide an elegant design detail. Look to some of the other stitch patterns for more edging ideas, such as shells or picots.

Single Crochet Edging

Working a row of single crochet stitches around a finished piece creates a neat, flat border.

1 Attach the yarn to the hook with a slip knot and join to a side of the piece.

Note: See Chapters 3 and 4 for more on slip knots and joining new yarn.

2 Work a single crochet stitch into each stitch or row across. Work 2 to 3 single crochets into the corner stitch; experiment to create a corner to your liking.

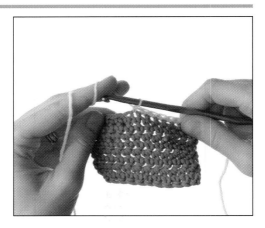

③ Repeat step 2 until you have completed your border. Fasten off and weave in the ends.

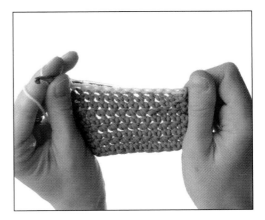

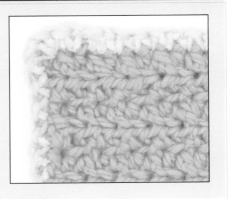

Make a Picot Edging

Picot edgings are widely used to add an elegant, feminine detail to crochet work.

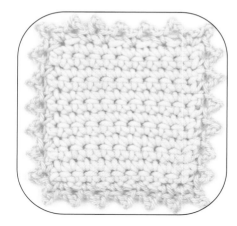

Picot Edging

1. Attach the yarn to the hook with a slip knot and join to a corner of the piece.

   Note: *See Chapters 3 and 4 for more on slip knots and joining new yarn.*

2. Work 1 single crochet into the next stitch.

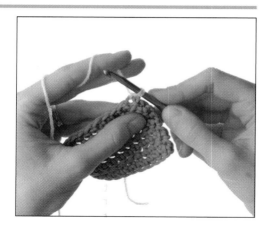

3 Chain 3.

4 Slip stitch into the first chain.

5 Skip 1 stitch; work a single crochet into the next stitch.

6 Repeat steps 3 and 4 to create a picot edging.

TIP

Work 5 chains to create a larger picot. You may need to skip 2 stitches before working the next single crochet to make the edging lay flat. Experiment!

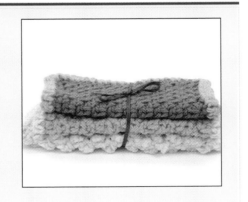

Make Pompoms

Pompoms add a playful embellishment on crocheted items, especially for kids. Place them on top of hats, at the ends of cords, or anywhere else that could use a little pizzazz.

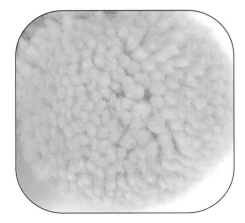

Pompoms

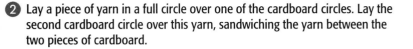

1. Cut two pieces of cardboard into circles the same size you want your pompom to be. Cut a pie piece out of each circle; then cut a circle out of the center of each of the circles. The two pieces should be identical.

2. Lay a piece of yarn in a full circle over one of the cardboard circles. Lay the second cardboard circle over this yarn, sandwiching the yarn between the two pieces of cardboard.

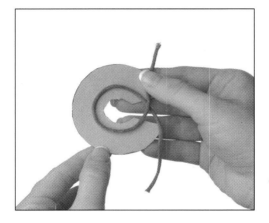

③ Hold the 2 circles together. Wrap yarn around the circle about 50 times—or more if you want a really fluffy pompom.

④ Using sharp scissors, cut the yarn between the 2 circles.

Tie the yarn sandwiched between the two cardboard circles into a very tight knot; this will cause the pompom to flare out.

⑤ Trim the ends of the pompoms so that they are uniform and neat.

Fringe is most often used to adorn afghans and scarves, but you can use fringe creatively to add a playful or elegant detail to hats, shawls, belts, and more.

Fringe

1. Cut a piece of cardboard that is slightly longer than the fringe you want to make. The piece of cardboard should be at least 3 or 4 inches wide.

   Note: A CD jewel case works well, too, just like in the photo!

2. Wrap the yarn around the cardboard or jewel case lengthwise. This ensures that all pieces of the fringe are the same length without requiring the tedious measurement of each strand.

3. Secure a rubber band around the cardboard or jewel case. (After you've cut the fringe, this rubber band will keep the pieces under control until you're ready to use them.) Cut the yarn along the bottom of the cardboard or jewel case. Keep the yarn folded in half.

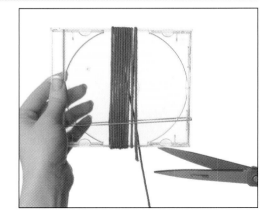

④ Insert the hook from back to front through the edge stitch to be fringed. Grab the middle of the folded fringe yarn and bring about 1 inch of the middle of the fringe through the stitch.

⑤ Use the hook to grab the entire bunch of fringe.
⑥ Draw the fringe through the loop.

⑦ Trim the ends of the fringe so that they are uniform.

Block Your Finished Project

Crocheted pieces made from natural fibers like cotton, wool, and silk look their best after they have been blocked to the proper shape and dimension. Blocking also helps make crochet stitches look uniform and even.

How to Block

If you are constructing an item from several crocheted pieces, it is generally recommended that you block the pieces separately before assembling them.

You need a firm, flat surface to serve as a blocking board on which to pin your pieces. You can use a bed, lay several towels on a table or carpet, or use a large Styrofoam board.

① Lay your crocheted pieces out on your blocking board (as shown in photo). Using your pattern as a guide, pin the pieces to the required shape and dimension.

Be sure to use rustproof pins.

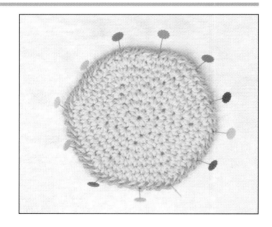

② Use a spray bottle to wet the pieces thoroughly, yet not to the point of saturation. Allow the pieces to dry.

As an alternative to spraying, you can steam your pieces to block them. Use the steam from an iron or a steamer held several inches above the pieces. Allow the pieces to dry as described previously.

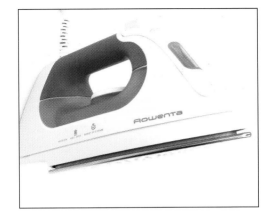

TIP

Unless your pattern specifically called for it, do not iron your crocheted pieces under any circumstances.

Simple Rectangles

A crocheted rectangle can be turned into a wide variety of useful, fun projects. Each pattern in this chapter starts with a crocheted rectangle. Let these projects spark your imagination. You'll be experimenting with stitch patterns and designing your own rectangle projects in no time!

Explore the Possibilities of the Rectangle

Whatever your comfort level with crochet, you simply need to know how to make a foundation chain and work rows of any stitch to make a unique and useful item.

What Can I Do with a Rectangle?

Take a rectangular piece of paper and imagine that it's a rectangle of crocheted fabric. Fold the paper in half and visualize the following:

- Seam two sides, fill the inside, and sew the top to make a pillow.
- Seam two sides and attach handles to make a purse.
- Seam two sides to make a hat.

Fold the paper in thirds to create a purse with a flap.

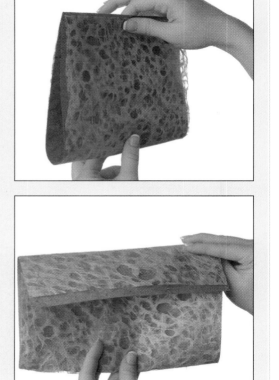

Scarves, most shawls, and many ponchos consist of one or more rectangles or squares. To make a squarish poncho, fold the rectangle in half and seam the sides, leaving a neck hole (like the project "It's a Shawl and a Poncho" in Chapter 14).

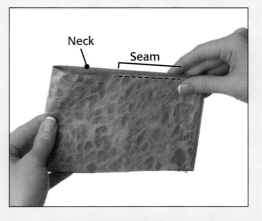

To make a pointed poncho, fold the rectangle into a cone shape and seam the ends (see photo).

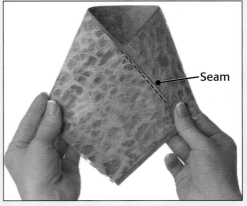

Simple Sampler Scarf

Practice basic stitches with this sampler scarf. Make the scarf with the suggested hook for a dense fabric, or try a larger hook for a looser look. You can modify the width and length of your scarf so that it fits just right.

Specifications

MATERIALS

Soft Cotton by Lana Grossa (60% cotton, 40% microfiber; 82 yds per 50 g), 2–4 skeins in color #21, blue

6.5 mm hook

TECHNIQUES USED

CH Chain

SC Single crochet

HDC Half double crochet

DC Double crochet

TR Treble crochet

Note: *See Chapter 3 for information about these techniques.*

FINISHED SIZE

Width: 4–5 inches. It's easy to change the width if you wish. Simply make a longer or shorter foundation chain!

Length: For a scarf that wraps once around your neck and stops at your hips, make a scarf as tall as your shoulders. To make a longer scarf, work until the length is equal to your height.

GAUGE

10 stitches = 4 inches

5 rows = 3 inches

Make the Simple Sampler Scarf

1 CH 18.

2 Row 1: Work 1 TR into fifth CH from hook and into each CH across; CH 1 and turn.

3 Row 2: Work 1 SC into first st of row and into each st across; CH 3 and turn.

4 Row 3: The turning CH counts as a DC. Work 1 DC into second st of row and into each CH across; CH 1 and turn.

5 Row 4: Work 1 SC into first st of row and into each st across; CH 2 and turn.

6 Row 5: Work 1 HDC into first st of row and into each st across; CH 1 and turn.

7 Repeat rows 1–5 until the scarf reaches the desired length. Fasten off and weave in ends.

Stretched Taffy Scarf

Start with a very long chain and work long rows to create this variation on a simple scarf. Changing colors in the middle makes a long stripe, like stretched taffy!

Specifications

MATERIALS

Soft Cotton by Lana Grossa (60% cotton, 40% microfiber; 82 yds per 50 g), 2 skeins in color #23, pink (yarn A), and 1 skein in color #1, white (yarn B)

6.5 mm hook

TECHNIQUES USED

CH Chain

ESC Extended single crochet

DTR Double treble crochet

Note: *See Chapters 3 and 5 for information about these techniques.*

FINISHED SIZE

Width: It's up to you! Work fewer repeats of row 2 for a skinny scarf; work more for a wider scarf.

Length: For this scarf, you can wrap the chain around your neck to see if it's long enough.

GAUGE

9 stitches = 4 inches

2 rows of ESC = 1 inch

Make the Stretched Taffy Scarf

1 Using yarn A, make a chain the length you desire for a perfect fit.

2 Row 1: Work 1 ESC into second CH from hook and into each CH across; CH 1 and turn.

3 Row 2: Work 1 ESC into first st of row and into each st across; CH 2 and turn.

4 Repeat row 2 until the scarf is a little shy of half the width you've planned. At the end of the last row, change to yarn B, CH 5, and turn. (See Chapter 4 for more on changing colors.)

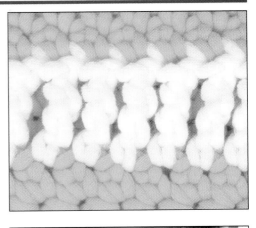

5 Row 3: The turning CH counts as the first DTR. Work 1 DTR into second st of row and into every CH across; change to yarn A, CH 2, and turn.

6 Repeat row 2 the same number of times as for the first half of the scarf, or work a few rows less for an asymmetrical look. Fasten off and weave in ends.

Exquisite Washcloths

This is an excellent pattern for practicing new stitches. A handmade washcloth is a true luxury, and this quick project makes a thoughtful gift, too.

Specifications

MATERIALS

Organic Cotton by Blue Sky Alpacas (100% cotton; 150 yds per 100 g), 1 skein in Nut (yarn A)

Dyed Cotton by Blue Sky Alpacas (100% cotton; 150 yds per 100 g), 1 skein in Shell (yarn B)

Dyed Cotton by Blue Sky Alpacas (100% cotton; 150 yds per 100 g), 1 skein in Thistle (yarn C)

Cotton Chenille by Crystal Palace Yarns (100% mercerized cotton; 98 yds per 50 g), 1 skein in color #1015, color? (yarn D)

5.5 mm hook

TECHNIQUES USED

CH Chain stitch

SC Single crochet

TR Treble crochet

HDC Half double crochet

FLO Front loop only

BLO Back loop only

Crunchy dots stitch pattern

Granite stitch pattern

Note: *See Chapters 3, 6, and 8 for information about these techniques.*

FINISHED SIZE

Sumptuous: 7½ inches x 6 ¾ inches

Crunchy Dots: 8 inches x 7½ inches

Granite: 7 inches x 6½ inches

GAUGE

Sumptuous: 14 HDC x 8 rows = 4 inches

Crunchy dots: 12 stitches x 10 rows = 4 inches

Granite: 15 stitches x 14 rows = 4 inches

Make the Washcloths

HALF DOUBLE CROCHET WASHCLOTH

① Using yarn D, CH 24.

② Row 1: Work 1 HDC into third CH from hook and into every CH across; CH 2 and turn.

③ Row 2: Work 1 HDC in FLO of first st. *Work 1 HDC in BLO of next st. Work 1 HDC in FLO of next st. Repeat from * across row. CH 2 and turn.

④ Repeat row 2 for 11 more rows or until the washcloth is the desired size. Fasten off.

⑤ Join yarn B a few sts before a corner. *Work 1 SC in each st along row; work 2 SC to turn corner; work 1 SC into each space along side, and work 2 to turn corner. Repeat from * to complete the border.

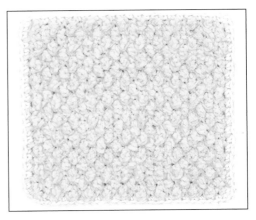

CRUNCHY DOTS WASHCLOTH

① Using yarn D, CH 25.

② Row 1: Work 1 SC in second CH from hook; *work 1 SC in next CH; work 1 TR in next CH. Repeat from * across to last CH. SC in last CH; CH 1 and turn.

③ Row 2: Work 1 SC in first st. *Work 1 SC in next st; work 1 TR in next st. Repeat from * to last st of row; work 1 SC in last st. CH 1 and turn.

④ Repeat row 2 for 18 more rows or until the washcloth is the desired size.

⑤ Join yarn B a few sts before a corner. *Work 1 SC in each st along row; work 2 SC to turn corner; work 1 SC into each space along side; and work 2 SC to turn corner. Repeat from * to complete the border.

GRANITE STITCH WASHCLOTH

① Using yarn C, CH 24.

② Row 1: Work 1 SC into second CH from hook. *Work 1 SC into next CH, CH 1, and skip 1 CH. Repeat from * until 2 CHs remain. CH 1, skip 1 CH, and work 1 SC into last CH. CH 1 and turn.

③ Row 2: Work 1 SC into first st. *Work 1 SC into next CH SP, CH 1, and skip 1 st. Repeat from * to end of row. Work 1 SC into last st. CH 1 and turn.

④ Repeat row 2 for 18 more rows or until the washcloth is the desired size.

⑤ Join yarn A a few sts before a corner. *Work 1 SC in each st along row; work 2 SC to turn corner; work 1 SC into each space along side; and work 2 to turn corner. Repeat from * to complete the border.

Cool Baby Hat

Practice your intarsia skills by adding this simple color patterning. Just make a rectangle, fold it in half, seam the two sides, and find a baby to wear it!

Specifications

MATERIALS

New Cotton by Lana Grossa (60% cotton, 40% microfiber; 88 yds per 50 g), 2 skeins in color #12, mulberry, and 1 skein in color #2, orange

4.5 mm hook

TECHNIQUES USED

CH Chain

SC Single crochet

Intarsia

Note: *See Chapters 3 and 11 for information about these techniques.*

FINISHED SIZE

Circumference: Approximately 20 inches

GAUGE

14 SC x 18 rows = 4 inches

Make the Cool Baby Hat

1. Create small balls of yarn to use as bobbins that can easily be left to hang as you switch between colors.

Yarn A	50 feet of mulberry
Yarn B	9 feet of orange
Yarn C	85 feet of mulberry
Yarn D	23 feet of orange
Yarn E	work from the skein of mulberry

2. Leaving a 12-inch tail (to be used later for seaming), CH 34 for the foundation CH.

3. Row 1: Using yarn A, work 1 SC into second CH from hook, work 1 SC into each CH across row, CH 1, and turn.

Follow the chart:

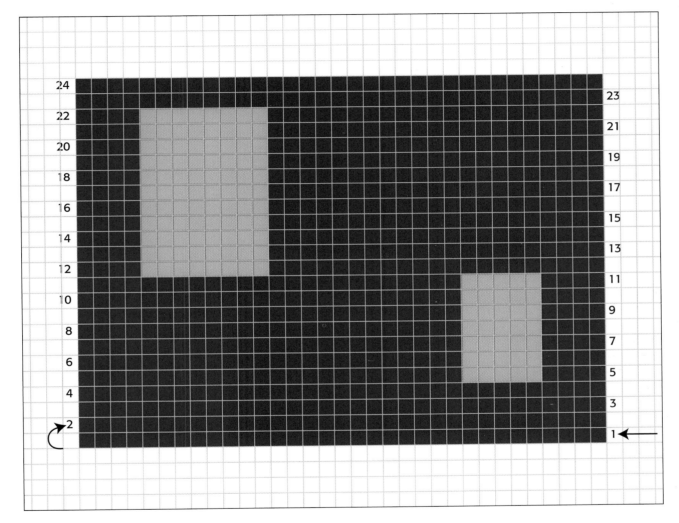

CONTINUED ON NEXT PAGE

④ Rows 2–4: Work 1 SC into each st across row. CH 1 and turn.

⑤ Row 5: Work 1 SC into each of the next 4 sts. Change to yarn B (see Chapter 4) and work the next 5 SC in yarn B. Change to yarn C and work 1 SC into each st to end of row. CH 1 and turn.

⑥ Row 6: Work 1 SC into each of the next 24 sts. Change to yarn B and work the next 5 SC in yarn B. Change to yarn A and work 1 SC into each st to end of row. CH 1 and turn.

⑦ Rows 7–11: Continue to follow the chart.

⑧ Row 12: Work 1 SC into each of the next 4 sts. Change to yarn D and work 1 SC into each of the next 8 sts. Change to yarn E and work 1 SC into each of the next 4 sts. CH 1 and turn.

⑨ Row 13: Work 1 SC into each of the next 21 sts. Change to yarn D and work 1 SC into each of the next 8 sts. Change to yarn C and work 1 SC into each st to the end of the row. CH 1 and turn.

⑩ Row 14: Work 1 SC into each of the next 4 sts. Change to yarn D and work 1 SC into each of the next 8 sts. Change to yarn E and work 1 SC into each st to the end of the row. CH 1 and turn.

⑪ Rows 15–22: Continue to follow the chart.

⑫ Row 23: Work 1 SC into each st across row. CH 1 and turn. Tie off, leaving a 12-inch tail.

⑬ Rows 24–48: Work 1 SC into each st across the row. CH 1 and turn.

⑭ Fasten off, leaving a 12-inch tail.

⑮ Fold the finished rectangle in half with the crocheted rows running widthwise.

⑯ Use the tail from the beginning and end of the rectangle to sew up each side.

Note: *If the hat is too big, simply tuck the sides in from the seams and use a whipstitch to secure the tuck.*

Made with a soft, washable yarn, this fun noisemaker is cushy and soft, too! You use a chained strap to secure toy rings around the noisemaker, making it easy for little hands to hold.

Specifications

MATERIALS

New Cotton Print by Lana Grossa (60% cotton, 40% microfiber; 88 yds per 50 g), 1 ball in color #202 (yellow), 1 ball in color #203 (turquoise), 1 ball in color #202 (lavender), and 1 ball in color #204 (green)

4.5 mm hook

Tapestry needle

3-inch plastic or wooden child-safe rings suitable for teething (we used Fisher-Price Link-a-Doos)

Filler: cotton or fiberfill

Old sock or pair of tights

Jingle bell or noisemaker

TECHNIQUES USED

CH Chain

SC Single crochet

Trinity cluster: Work 3 SC TOG into same space as the last stitch and over the next 2 spaces

Trinity stitch pattern

Note: *See Chapters 3, 6, and 9 for information about these techniques.*

FINISHED SIZE

2¾ inches x 6½ inches

GAUGE

16 stitches x 16 rows = 4 inches

CONTINUED ON NEXT PAGE

Make the Noisemaker

1 CH 25.

2 Row 1: Work 1 SC into second CH from hook and into every CH across. CH 1 and turn.

3 Row 2: Work 1 SC into first st. Work 1 trinity cluster starting in same st as prev SC worked, and then into next 2 sts. *CH 1. Work 1 trinity cluster into same space as last st of prev cluster, and then into next 2 sts. Repeat from * across row. Work 1 SC into same space as last st of prev trinity cluster, CH 1, and turn.

4 Rows 3–6: Repeat row 2. At end of row 6, change to yarn B (turquoise).

5 Row 7: Repeat row 2. Change to yarn C (lavender) at end of row.

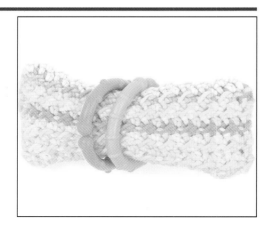

6 Rows 8–12: Repeat row 2. Change to yarn D (green) at end of row 12.

7 Row 13: Repeat row 2. Change to yarn A (yellow) at end of row 13.

8 Rows 14 and 15: Repeat row 2. Change to yarn B (turquoise) at end of row 15.

9 Row 16: Repeat row 2. Change to yarn A (yellow) at end of row 16.

10 Rows 17–21: Repeat row 2.

11 Fasten off, leaving a 12-inch tail for seaming.

FINISH THE NOISEMAKER

1 Fold the finished rectangle in half with the rows running widthwise.

2 Use the tail from the beginning and end of the rectangle to sew up one short side. Continue along to sew the long side, leaving the second short side open.

3 To use an old sock as a liner, keep the toe end of the sock and cut away whatever part of the sock won't fit in the noisemaker. Place the sock liner in the noisemaker.

4 Partially stuff with filler and a jingle bell or other small noisemaker. Sew sock shut.

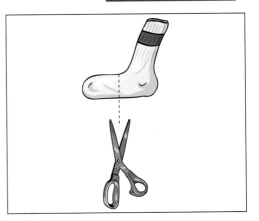

5 To secure the rings, CH 15. Weave 1 end of the chain through the crocheted fabric and over the rings. Tie the ends of the chain together.

6 Finish stuffing the noisemaker. Use the tail left on the open end to sew it closed. Weave in all tails.

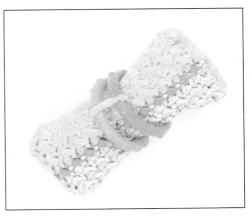

Precious Clutch Purse

You can easily make a basic rectangle into a fashionable purse. Crocheting with two complimentary yarns at the same time creates a unique fabric that is all your own. To do so, simply hold the two strands together and work as usual.

Specifications

MATERIALS

Caramella by Lana Grossa (50% cotton, 48% microfiber, 2% polyester; 88 yards per 50 g), 1 skein in color #012, white

Tratto by Lana Grossa (60% microfiber, 25% viscose, 15% linen; 110 yards per 50 g), 1 skein in color #008, pink

8 mm hook

Length of ribbon approximately 1 yd long

TECHNIQUES USED

CH Chain

SC Single crochet

FLO Front loop only

Seaming

Note: See Chapters 3, 6, and 11.

FINISHED SIZE

8½ inches x 10 inches

GAUGE

10 stitches x 7 rows = 4 inches

Make the Precious Clutch Purse

1. Leaving a long tail, and working with both yarns held together, CH 29.

2. Row 1: With 1 strand of each yarn held together, work 1 SC into second CH from hook and into every CH across. CH 1 and turn.

3. Row 2: Work 1 SC into FLO of every st across row. CH 1 and turn.

4. Repeat row 2 18 times.

5. Cut yarn, leaving a long tail.

6. Fold finished rectangle in half with rows running vertically.

FINISH THE PRECIOUS CLUTCH

1. Use the long tail from the beginning of the piece to sew one side of the rectangle using your preferred seaming technique. (See Chapter 12 for more on seaming.) Use the long tail from the end of the piece to sew the other side of the rectangle.

   Note: You are sewing the purse together inside out so that the knots and seams will be hidden. Continue to work on the inside of the purse until you are instructed to turn the purse out.

2. Turn the purse out.

LINE THE PRECIOUS CLUTCH

1. If you'd like to make a fabric lining, cut a rectangle of fabric the same size as the purse plus ¼ inch on each side for seams.

2. Fold rectangle and seam sides just as you did for the purse body.

3. Fold and hem top of lining.

4. Place lining inside purse and use sewing thread to whipstitch lining into purse.

FINISHING TOUCHES

1. Weave ribbon through stitches at top of purse.

2. Gently pull on each end of the ribbon to cinch and shape the top. Be careful to leave enough space to fit your hand into the purse. Make a pretty bow. Trim ribbon tails.

chapter 14

Patterns

The patterns in this chapter will help you explore the techniques and stitches you learned in previous chapters. Follow any pattern row by row, and you'll amaze yourself with what you can make!

Oval Trivet and Circular Coasters

Sometimes you're itching to crochet, but you just don't have the right yarn for the project. If you find yourself in this situation, walk into the kitchen and grab some kitchen twine. Now that you're in the kitchen, couldn't you use a new trivet? How about new coasters?

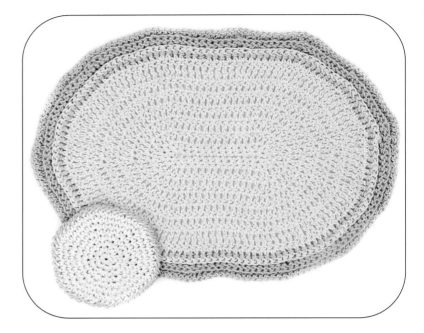

Specifications

MATERIALS

Trivet: approx. 100 yards cotton kitchen twine (yarn A)

Coaster: 12 yards cotton kitchen twine (yarn A)

4.50–5.50 mm hook, depending on the thickness of the twine

1 skein Patons *Grace* (100% mercerized cotton, 136 yards/50g) in Ginger (yarn B)

4.50 mm hook

TECHNIQUES USED

CH Chain

SC Single crochet

DC Double crochet

FPDC Front post double crochet

Note: *See Chapters 3, 4, and 11 for information about these techniques.*

FINISHED SIZE

Trivet: 15 inches x 10 inches

Coaster: 4½ inches round

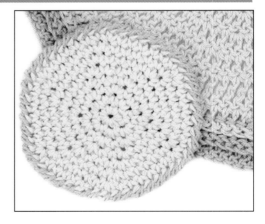

Make the Oval Trivet

This project involves working in the round to create an oval; the short ends are entirely round, and the longer sides are straight. (See "Work in the Round: Rows" in Chapter 4.)

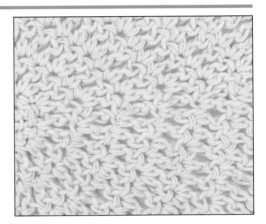

 With yarn A, CH 15.

② Round 1: Work 1 SC into top loop of second CH from hook. Continue to work 1 SC into each CH across, to last CH. Work 2 SC into last CH. Continue to work into backside (bottom loop) of CH, working into each CH across (28 SC total). Sl st into first st of rnd.

③ Round 2: CH 1. Work 2 SC into first st from prev rnd. Work 2 SC into next st. Work 1 SC into each of the next 10 sts. Work 2 SC into each of the next 4 sts. Work 1 SC into each of the next 10 sts. Work 2 SC into each of the next 2 sts. Sl st into first st of rnd.

④ Round 3: CH 3. This CH counts as 1 DC. Work 1 DC into first st and 2 DC into each of the next 2 sts. Work 1 DC into each of the next 12 sts, then 2 DC into each of the next 6 sts, and 1 DC into each of the next 12 sts. Work 2 DC into each of the last 3 sts. Sl st to third CH of turning CH from beg of rnd.

⑤ Round 4: CH 3; this CH counts as 1 DC. Work 1 DC into first st and 1 DC into next st. Work 2 DC into next st. Place a marker in the second of the 2 sts.

⑥ Work 1 DC into next st and work 2 DC into each of the next 2 sts. Place a marker in the second of each pair of sts.

⑦ Work 1 DC into each of the next 12 sts. Work 2 DC into each of the next 2 sts. Place a marker in the second of each pair of sts. Work 1 DC into next st and 2 DC into next st, twice. Place a marker in the second of each pair of sts.

⑧ Work 2 DC into next st and 1 DC into next st, twice. Place a marker in the first of each pair of sts.

⑨ Work 2 DC into each of the next 2 sts. Place a marker in the second of each pair of sts.

⑩ Work 1 DC into each of the next 12 sts.

⑪ Work 2 DC into each of the next 2 sts. Place a marker in the second of each pair of sts.

⑫ Work 1 DC into next st and 2 DC into next st, twice. Place a marker in the second of each pair of sts.

⑬ Work 2 DC into last st of rnd. Place a marker in the second of each pair of sts.

⑭ Sl st to third CH of turning CH from beg of rnd.

CONTINUED ON NEXT PAGE

15 Round 5: CH 3. This chain counts as 1 DC. Work 1 DC into first st. Work 1 DC into each unmarked st. Work 2 DC into each marked st. Move markers to the second of each pair of sts. Sl st to third CH of turning CH from beg of rnd.

16 Rep row 5 until the piece is the size you want.

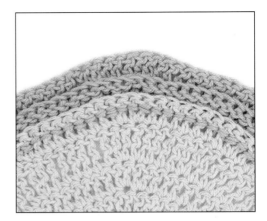

CREATE THE TRIVET BORDER

1 Change to yarn B and CH 4; this CH counts as 1 FPTR.

2 Work 1 FPTR into first st. Work FPTR into each unmarked st. Work 2 FPTR into each marked st. Move markers into second of each pair of sts. Sl st to third CH of turning CH from beg of rnd. Sl st to fourth CH of turning CH from beg of rnd.

TIP

It's easy to add variety to your oval:

- Mix in a yarn like Patons *Grace* to add stripes.
- Try a taller stitch such as double treble crochet for a round. Be careful to adjust your turning chain appropriately.

Make the Circular Coaster

You work this project in the round by using the spiral method to create quick, easy circles.

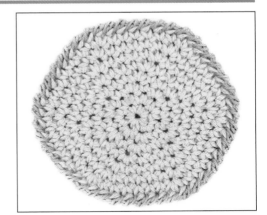

1 With yarn A, CH 2.

2 Round 1: Work 6 SC into second CH from hook. Mark first st with st marker.

3 Round 2: Work 2 SC into each st from prev rnd. Continue to move marker to indicate first st of every rnd.

4 Round 3: *Work 2 SC into next st from prev rnd and 1 SC into next st. Rep from * across rnd.

5 Round 4: *Work 2 SC into next st from prev rnd and 1 SC into each of the next 2 sts. Rep from * across rnd.

6 Round 5: *Work 2 SC into next st from prev rnd and 1 SC into each of the next 3 sts. Rep from * across rnd.

7 Round 6: *Work 2 SC into next st from prev rnd and 1 SC into each of the next 4 sts. Rep from * across rnd.

8 Round 7: *Work 2 SC into next st from prev rnd and 1 SC into each of the next 5 sts. Rep from * across rnd.

ADD THE EDGING

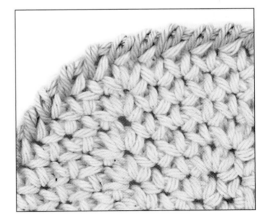

1 Join yarn B and work 1 crab st into each st across rnd. Sl st to first st of rnd to join.

2 Tie off and weave in ends.

Beanie

This warm, unisex beanie fits snugly for a stylish look. The extended single crochet stitch gives it a yummy texture. Turning your work an inch from the brim of the hat creates a subtle band.

When making a hat, it's easy to customize the fit. Work increase rows until the piece barely covers the crown of your head; then work even rows for a snug fit. To make a smaller hat, simply work fewer increase rows. To make a hat larger, work more increase rows.

Specifications

MATERIALS

1 hank Fleece Artist *Kid Aran* (50% kid/50% wool, 375 meters/250g) in Mahogany

5.50 mm hook

Stitch marker

TECHNIQUES USED

Adjustable ring

CH   Chain

Sl st Slip stitch

ESC   Extended single crochet

Note: *See Chapters 3, 4, and 5 for information about these techniques.*

FINISHED SIZE

One size fits most adult heads. See the pattern for advice on customizing the fit.

Circumference = 22 inches

GAUGE

12 stitches and 13 rows = 4 inches (10 cm) in ESC

Make the Beanie

Start with an adjustable ring. (See Chapter 4 for instructions.)

1 Round 1: Work 8 SC into ring; sl st into first SC to join rnd. Gently pull on tail to tighten ring. Mark first st with stitch marker and CH 2 (8 SC total).

2 Round 2: Work 1 ESC into same st the sl st is worked into. *Work 2 ESC in next SC. Rep from * until 1 st remains. Remove marker. Work 1 ESC in same st the first ESC was worked into; sl st into first ESC to join. Place marker in first st. Continue to move marker to indicate first st of every rnd. CH 2 (16 ESC total).

3 Round 3: Work 1 ESC into same st the sl st is worked into. Place marker in first st. Continue to move marker to indicate first st of every rnd. *Work 1 ESC into next st and 2 ESC into next st. Rep from * until 1 st remains. Work 1 ESC into next st. Work 1 ESC in same st the first ESC was worked into; sl st into first ESC to join. CH 1 (24 ESC total).

4 Round 4: Work 1 ESC into the same st the Sl st is worked into. *Work 1 ESC in each of the next 2 sts. Work 2 ESC into the next st. Rep from * until 1 st remains. Work 1 ESC into the next st. Work 1 ESC into the same st the first ESC was worked into. Sl st into the first ESC to join. CH 1 (32 ESC total).

5 Round 5: Work 1 ESC into same st the Sl st is worked into. *Work 1 ESC in each of the next 3 sts; work 2 ESC into next st. Rep from * until 1 st remains. Work 1 ESC into next st. Work 1 ESC into same st the first ESC was worked into. Sl st to first ESC to join. CH 1 (40 ESC total).

Note: *With each round, 1 more stitch is worked even between increases.*

6 Round 6: Work 1 ESC into same st the Sl st is worked into. *Work 1 ESC into each of the next 4 sts; work 2 ESC into next st. Rep from * until 1 st remains. Work 1 ESC into next st. Work 1 ESC into same st the first ESC was worked into. Sl st to first ESC to join. CH 1 (48 ESC total).

7 Round 7: Work 1 ESC into same st the Sl st is worked into. *Work 1 ESC into each of the next 5 sts; work 2 ESC into next st. Rep from * until 1 st remains. Work 1 ESC into next st. Work 1 ESC into same st the first ESC was worked into. Sl st to first ESC to join. CH 1 (56 ESC total).

SHAPE THE CROWN

1 Round 8: Work 1 ESC into same st the sl st is worked into. *Work 1 ESC into each of the next 14 sts; work 2 ESC into next st. Rep from * until 1 st remains. Work 1 ESC into next st. Work 1 ESC into same st the first ESC was worked into. Sl st into first ESC to join. CH 1 (60 ESC total).

2 Round 9: Work 1 ESC into same st the sl st is worked into. *Work 1 ESC into each of the next 15 sts; work 2 ESC into next st. Rep from * until 1 st remains. Work 1 ESC into next st. Work 1 ESC into same st the first ESC was worked into. Sl st into first ESC to join. CH 1 (64 ESC total).

3 Rounds 10–19: Work 1 ESC into each st around. Sl st into first ESC to join. CH 1 (64 ESC total).

TURN TO CREATE A SUBTLE BAND

1 Round 20: Turn. Work 1 ESC into each st around. Sl st into first ESC to join. CH 1 (64 ESC total).

2 Rounds 21–22: Work 1 ESC into each st around. Sl st into first ESC to join.

3 Tie off and weave in ends.

Cloche

Add a feminine touch to the beanie pattern with this sweet edging.

MATERIALS

1 hank Fleece Artist *Kid Silk* (70% kid/30% silk, 375 meters/250g) in Ruby Red

5.50 mm hook

Stitch marker

TECHNIQUES USED

Adjustable ring

CH   Chain

Sl st   Slip stitch

ESC   Extended single crochet

Note: *See Chapters 3, 4, and 5 for information about these techniques.*

Popcorn Dance pattern

Note: *See the Popcorn Dance pattern in Chapter 8.*

V-stitch: Work [1 DC, CH 2, 1 DC] into the same st.

Popcorn stitch: Work 4 DCs into the same st. Join through the top and CH 1. (See the section "Popcorns" in Chapter 7.)

Popcorn V-stitch: Work [1 DC, CH 2, and 1 popcorn st] all into the same st.

FINISHED SIZE

One size fits most adult heads

Circumference = 22 inches

GAUGE

12 stitches and 13 rows = 4 inches (10 cm) in ESC

Make the Cloche

1 Rounds 1–8: ork the preceding beanie pattern through round 8 (60 ESC total).

2 Rounds 9–19: Work 1 ESC into each st around. Sl st into first ESC to join. CH 1 (60 ESC total).

MAKE THE EDGING

1 Edging round 1: CH 3. Starting in second st of rnd, *work 1 popcorn V-stitch, skip 2 sts, and work 1 V-stitch. Rep from * around until 5 sts remain. Skip 2 sts and work [1 DC, CH 2] into next st. Sl st into top CH of the CH 3 at beg of rnd.

2 Edging round 2: CH 3. *Work 1 V-stitch into next CH 2 space. Work 1 popcorn V-stitch into next CH 2 space. Rep from * around. Sl st into top CH of the CH 3 at beg of rnd.

3 Fasten off and weave in ends.

Sweet and Chic Granny Square Bag

Granny squares are easy, cheery, and quick to stitch. Combine a rich yarn, such as Crystal Palace Cotton Chenille, with sweet colors and a traditional navy to create a bag that is both old-fashioned and irresistibly chic.

Specifications

MATERIALS

Crystal Palace Cotton Chenille (100% cotton, 98 yards/50g):

- 2 skeins in #4272 Navy
- 1 skein in #7366 Rose
- 1 skein in #1015 Ecru
- 1 skein in #5638 Ice Blue
- 1 skein in #1240 Lime Green
- 1 skein in #2230 Pumpkin
- 1 skein in #7684 Antique Brown

5.50 mm hook

TECHNIQUES USED

Adjustable ring

SC   Single crochet

FLO   Front loop only

Granny square pattern

Note: *See Chapters 3, 4, and 9 for information about these techniques.*

FINISHED SIZE

21 inches wide x 7 inches tall x 3½ inches deep

GAUGE

To be determined

Make the Granny Square Bag

TO BEGIN

You will make six squares in total. Each square includes three rounds of the Granny Square pattern and a border. Make 2 squares in each color combination:

Square 1:

Round 1: Ice Blue
Round 2: Antique Brown
Round 3: Lime Green

Square 2:

Round 1: Ice Blue
Round 2: Antique Brown
Round 3: Lime Green

Square 3:

Round 1: Lime Green
Round 2: Ecru
Round 3: Rose

1 Round 1: Using an adjustable ring, CH 3. Work 2 DC into ring. *CH 2 and work 3 DC into ring. Rep from * twice to create 2 more granny clusters. CH 2, Sl st into third CH of the CH 3 at beg of rnd. Tie off.

2 Round 2: Join yarn in next CH 2 space. Work [CH 3, 2 DC, CH 2, 3 DC] into CH space. *CH 1. In next CH space, work a corner set [CH 2, 3 DC, CH 2, 3 DC]. Rep from * to work a corner set into each CH 2 space. Sl st into third CH of the CH 3 at beg of rnd. Tie off.

3 Round 3: Join yarn in next corner CH space. Work [CH 3, 2 DC, CH 2, 3 DC] into CH space. *CH 1. Work 1 granny cluster in next CH 1 space; CH 1. In next CH 2 space, work a corner set [CH 2, 3 DC, CH 2, 3 DC]. Rep from * twice to work into each CH space. Sl st in third chain of the CH 3 at beg of rnd.

4 Fasten off and weave in ends.

CROCHET A BORDER AROUND EACH SQUARE

1 Round 4: Join ice blue yarn, CH 3, and work 1 DC into each st and side space from prev rnd. Work [2 DC, CH 2, 2 DC] into corner spaces.

2 Round 5: Join navy yarn, CH 1, and work 1 SC into each st from prev rnd. Work [1 SC, CH 1, 1 SC] into each corner. Sl st to first st of rnd and CH 1.

3 Round 6: Rep rnd 5.

4 Fasten off and weave in ends.

CONTINUED ON NEXT PAGE

MAKE THE BODY

1 CH 10.

2 Row 1: Work 1 SC into each CH across. CH 1 and turn.

3 Row 2: Work 1 SC into each st from prev row. CH 1 and turn.

4 Rows 3–22: Rep row 2.

5 Row 23: Work 1 SC into FLO of each st from prev row. CH 1 and turn.

6 Row 24: Place stitch marker in this row. Work 1 SC into BLO of each st from prev row. CH 1 and turn.

7 Row 25: Work 1 SC into FLO of each st from prev row. CH 1 and turn.

8 Rows 26–89: Rep row 2.

9 Row 90: Work 1 SC into FLO of each st from prev row. CH 1 and turn.

10 Row 91: Place stitch marker in this row. Work 1 SC into BLO of each st from prev row. CH 1 and turn.

11 Row 92: Work 1 SC into FLO of each st from prev row. CH 1 and turn.

12 Rows 93–115: Rep row 2.

13 Fasten off and weave in ends.

MAKE THE HANDLES

Use leftover yarn from the squares to create striped handles, switching colors with each row.

1 CH 41.

2 Row 1: Work 1 SC into each CH across. CH 1 and turn.

3 Rows 2–5: Work 1 SC into each SC from prev row. CH 1 and turn.

4 To shape the handle, fold in half lengthwise. Seam first and last rows to each other by using SC; join yarn at tenth stitch of the rows. Work 20 SC across.

5 Fasten off and weave in ends, leaving a tail on each end for seaming.

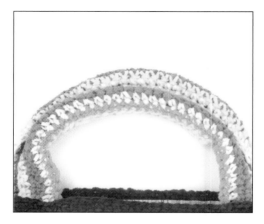

FINISH THE BAG

Join the squares to create 2 side panels for the purse:

1 Whipstitch 3 squares together to create 1 side panel.

2 Whipstitch rem 3 squares together to create other side panel.

Note: *See Chapter 12 for more on seaming.*

Edge each panel with more SC:

3 Join navy yarn and CH 1. Work 1 SC into each st from prev rnd. Work [1 SC, CH 1, 1 SC] into each corner. Place stitch marker in each CH 1 corner space. Sl st into first st of rnd.

Seam body to granny square panels:

4 With right sides facing outward, match marked corners of 1 panel with marked rows of body. Join navy yarn at one end and SC panel to body.

Note: *This single crochet seam will be on the outside of the purse. This detail gives the purse a tailored look.*

5 Rep with second panel and other side of body strip.

6 Whipstitch handles to inside of panels.

LINE THE BAG

Because the granny squares create a fabric with open spaces, the lining is an important part of this bag's look and feel. Have fun choosing a fabric that reflects your own style!

1 Cut a piece of fabric that's 26 inches x 20 inches.

2 Cut fabric as shown to create a notch on each side.

3 Fold and iron creases to shape bottom of lining.

4 Fold and iron creases to shape each side of lining.

5 Sew each side.

6 Fold and iron creases to shape top of lining.

7 Place lining in bag. Pin lining into place, aligning corners and creases with corresponding parts of bag.

8 Sew lining into place. To keep stitches from showing through on the outside of the purse, sew halfway through each crocheted stitch.

Note: *See Chapter 11 for more on seaming.*

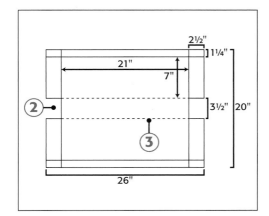

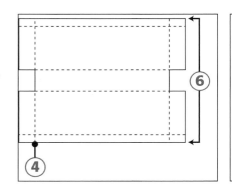

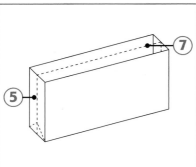

Round Box

Inspired by a lip balm tin, this little round box is perfect for keeping small secrets inside. This versatile pattern can be crocheted with any yarn to create boxes of different sizes.

MATERIALS

1 skein Fonty *Majorque* (60% cotton/40% linen, 135 yards/50g) in #136 (Pink)

2.75 mm hook

TECHNIQUES USED

CH Chain

Sl st Slip stitch

SC Single crochet

FLO Front loop only

Working rounds in rows

Note: *See Chapters 3 and 4 for information about these techniques.*

FINISHED SIZE

Lid: 1¾ inches wide x ⅜ inch deep

Body: 1½ inches wide by ¾ inch deep

GAUGE

6 stitches and 7 rows = 1 inch (4 cm) in single crochet

Make the Round Box

MAKE THE BOTTOM

❶ Start with an adjustable ring. (See Chapter 4 for instructions.)

❷ Round 1: Work 6 SC into ring. Sl st into first SC to join rnd. Gently pull on tail to tighten ring. CH 1 and turn (6 SC total).

❸ Round 2: Work 2 SC into first SC. *Work 2 SC into next SC. Rep from * 4 more times. Sl st into first SC to join. CH 1 and turn (12 SC total).

❹ Round 3: Work 2 SC into first SC and 1 SC into next SC. *Work 2 SC into next SC and 1 SC into next SC. Rep from * 4 more times. Sl st into first SC to join. CH 1 and turn (18 SC total).

⑤ Round 4: Work 2 SC into first SC and 1 SC into each of the next 2 SC. *Work 2 SC into next SC and 1 SC into each of the next 2 SC. Rep from * 4 more times. Sl st into first SC to join. CH 1 and turn (24 SC total).

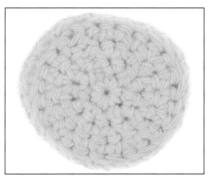

⑥ Round 5: Work 1 SC into FLO of each st from prev rnd. Sl st into first SC to join. CH 1 and turn (24 SC total).

Note: *Working in the front loop only in this row creates a ridge to form the bend.*

⑦ Round 6: Work 1 SC into each st from prev round. Sl st into first SC to join. CH 1 and turn (24 SC total).

⑧ Round 7: Work 1 SC into each st from prev rnd. Sl st to first SC to join. CH 1, but do not turn (24 SC total).

Note: *Whether a round is turned or not affects the texture of the fabric. This effect is used to create a slight ridge that the lid rests on.*

⑨ Round 8: Work 1 SC into each st from prev rnd. Sl st to first SC to join. CH 1, but do not turn (24 SC total).

⑩ Round 9: Work 1 SC into each st from prev round. Sl st to first SC to join. CH 1 and turn (24 SC total).

⑪ Fasten off and weave in ends.

MAKE THE LID

① Work rounds 1–4 as you did for the body.

② Round 5: Work 2 SC into first SC. Work 1 SC into each of the next 3 SC. *Work 2 SC into next SC and 1 SC into each of the next 3 SC. Rep from * 4 more times. Sl st to first SC to join. CH 1 and turn (30 SC total).

③ Round 6: Work 1 SC into FLO of each st from prev rnd. Sl st to first SC to join. CH 1 and turn (30 SC total).

④ Round 7: Work 1 SC into each st from prev rnd. Sl st to first SC to join. CH 1 and turn (30 SC total).

⑤ Round 8: Work 1 SC into each st from prev rnd. Sl st to first SC to join (30 SC total).

⑥ Fasten off and weave in ends.

 TIP

Try adding beads to dress up the lid. We added beads to every other stitch of round 4.

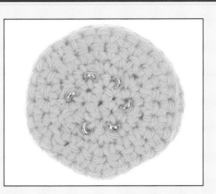

Tunisian Tie

Have you ever felt like it's hard to find terrific projects to make for the men in your life? Polish your Tunisian crochet skills while you work up this simple necktie. The woven-like fabric makes for a unique and office-appropriate accessory.

Specifications

MATERIALS

1 hank Knit Picks *Sock Landscape* (100% merino wool, 192 yds/50g) in Yukon

4.5 mm Tunisian crochet hook

TECHNIQUES USED

CH   Chain

Tss   Tunisian simple stitch

inc   Increase

dec   Decrease

Note: *See Chapters 3 and 10 for information about these techniques.*

FINISHED SIZE

One size fits most adults

GAUGE

24 stitches and 21 rows = 4 inches (10 cm) in Tss

Make the Tunisian Tie

BEGIN THE TUNISIAN TIE

1. CH 19.

2. Foundation forward row: Pick up 1 loop in second CH from hook. Pick up 1 loop in each CH across.

3. Foundation return row: CH 1. *YO and draw through 2 loops on hook. Rep from * until 1 loop remains on hook at end of return row (18 Tss total).

4. Forward row: Pick up 1 loop in each vertical bar.

5. Return row: CH 1. *YO and draw through 2 loops on hook. Rep from * until 1 loop remains on hook at end of return row.

6. Rep pairs of forward and return rows until tie measures 10 inches from beg.

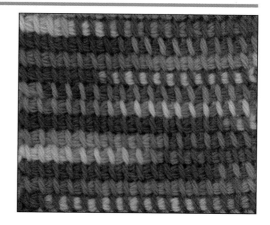

DECREASE

1. On next forward row, decrease 1 st on each end of row. Work return row as normal (16 Tss total).

2. Continue to decrease 1 st on each end of forward rows every 22 rows until piece measures 26 inches (9 sts total). Work even for 30 inches until piece measures 56 inches.

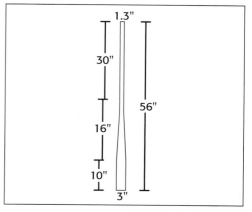

WORK THE FINAL ROW

1. Work Tunisian bind-off row (see Chapter 11). Tie off and weave in ends.

2. Block to combat curl at either end (see Chapter 12).

   If your tie still curls, make a single crochet or slip stitch border to add structure.

It's a Shawl and a Poncho

This pattern creates a shawl that can also be attached at the side and worn as a poncho. The Odd Shells pattern from Chapter 9 is worked with a larger hook than the yarn calls for, creating a flowing, lacy drape.

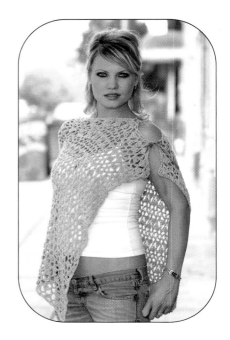

Specifications

MATERIALS

5–7 skeins Elsebeth Lavold *Silky Tweed* (40% silk/30% cotton/20% merino wool/10% viscose, 132 yards/50g) in #09 Flax

6 mm hook

TECHNIQUES USED

CH   Chain

Sl st Slip stitch

SC   Single crochet

V-stitch: Work [1 DC, CH 2, 1 DC] into the same stitch

Odd V-stitch: Work [2 DC, CH 2, 1 DC] into the same stitch

Note: See Chapters 3 and 9 for information about these techniques.

FINISHED SIZE

See the instructions in the pattern to size your shawl.

GAUGE

1 repeat of pattern = 4 inches

6 rows = 4 inches

Make the Shawl or Poncho

DETERMINE HOW BIG TO MAKE YOUR SHAWL

To get an accurate measurement, get a friend to help you!

1. Measure from the center of your neck to your wrist bone. Multiply this number by 2 for the length you need. Continue to work rows until the piece measures this length.

2. Measure from the top of your shoulder to your wrist. This is the width you need. Use this width to determine how many repeats of the pattern to use in each row.

   1 repeat of the pattern = 4 inches. For a width of 28 inches, crochet 7 repeats of the pattern.

   Foundation chain: Each repeat of the pattern is a multiple of 8 chains:
   7 x 8 = 56.

CROCHET THE SHAWL

The foundation chain for this pattern consists of a multiple of 8 + 2 + 1. Multiply the number of repeats you are working by 8, and then add 2, plus 1 more for the turning chain.

1. Row 1: Work 1 SC into second CH from hook and 1 SC into each CH across. CH 1 and turn.

2. Row 2: Work 1 V-st into second st, skip 2 sts, and work 1 Odd V-st into next st. *Skip 2 sts and work 1 V-st into next st. Skip 2 sts and work 1 Odd V-st into next st. Rep from * to last 2 sts and work 1 DC into last st. CH 3 and turn.

3. Row 3: *Work 1 Odd V-st into CH 2 space and 1 V-st into next CH 2 space. Rep from * to end of row. Work 1 DC into space between turning CH and DC of prev row. CH 3 and turn.

4. Row 4: *Work 1 V-st into CH 2 space and 1 Odd V-st into next CH 2 space. Rep from * to end of row. Work 1 DC into space between turning CH and DC of prev row. CH 3 and turn.

5. Rep rows 3 and 4 to desired length. Tie off and weave in ends.

TURN THE SHAWL INTO A PONCHO

1. Fold shawl in half lengthwise.

2. If you wish to be able to switch between wearing this piece as a shawl and a poncho, attach with ribbons, a brooch, or buttons along the side. The open fabric makes it so that you don't need buttonholes.

   Seam the sides together to create a permanent poncho.

Bold Bag

Certain circumstances call for a bold, sturdy bag. This bag is worked in one piece and doesn't require seaming or lining. Fulling the completed bag adds structure, strength, and texture.

Specifications

MATERIALS

Yarn A: 4 skeins Rio de la Plata *Wool Solid* (100% wool, 140 yards/99g) in Sparkling Grape

Yarn B: 1 skein Rio de la Plata *Wool Solid* (100% wool, 140 yards/99g) in Natural White

8.00 mm hook

TECHNIQUES USED

CH   Chain

Sl st Slip stitch

SC   Single crochet

Working rounds in rows

3 SC TOG   3 single crochets worked together

Fulling

Note: *See Chapters 3, 4, and 10 for information about these techniques.*

FINISHED SIZE

Before fulling: 22 inches wide x 15 inches tall x 6 inches deep

After fulling: 17 inches x 11 inches

GAUGE

10 single crochets and 12 rows = 4 inches (10 cm), before fulling

Make the Bold Bag

MAKE THE BOTTOM OF THE BAG

1 With yarn A, CH 43.

2 Row 1: Work 1 SC into second CH from hook and into each CH across. CH 1 and turn.

3 Row 2: Work 1 SC into each st from prev row. CH 1 and turn.

4 Rows 3–18: Rep row 2.

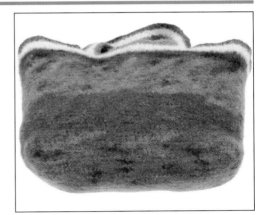

MAKE THE PURSE BODY

1 Round 1: Work 1 SC into each st from prev row. Work 3 SC into last st of row to create a corner, place marker in middle st of corner. Work 1 SC into each row along side of rectangle. Work 3 SC to create a corner, place marker in middle st of corner. Work 1 SC into each st from foundation row. Work 3 SC to create a corner, place marker in middle st of corner. Work 1 SC into each row along side of rectangle. Work 2 SC and sl st to first SC of rnd to create a corner, place marker in middle st of corner. CH 1.

2 Round 2: *Work 1 SC into each st from prev rnd. Work 3 SC into marked st. Rep from * to end of row. CH 1.

3 Round 3: Work 1 SC into each st from prev rnd. CH 1.

4 Rounds 4–38: Rep rnd 3.

5 Round 39: Work 1 SC into each st from prev rnd. Change to yarn B and CH 1.

Note: See Chapter 11 for information about changing colors.

6 Round 40: Work 1 SC into each st from prev rnd. CH 1.

7 Round 41: Rep rnd 40.

CONTINUED ON NEXT PAGE

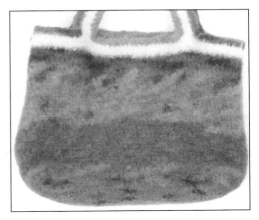

MAKE THE HANDLES

1 Lay bag flat and place marker 8 inches in from the outside on each side of bag. Flip bag over and place marker 8 inches in from the outside on each side of bag.

2 Round 42: Work 1 SC into each st from prev rnd until you reach first marker. CH 38 and work 1 SC into st after second marker. Work 1 SC into each st from prev rnd, until you reach third marker. CH 38 and work 1 SC into st after fourth marker. Work 1 SC into each st from prev rnd. CH 1.

3 Round 43: Work 1 SC into each SC from prev rnd; work 1 SC into each CH from handle sections as well. Change to yarn A and CH 1.

Note: *See Chapter 4 for information about changing yarns.*

4 Rounds 44–45: Work 1 SC into each st from prev rnd. CH 1.

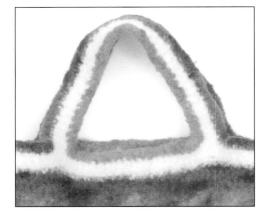

FINISH THE HANDLES

1 Place markers at inside corners of handles.

2 Handle round 1: Using yarn B, join into unworked side of handle chain. Work 1 SC into unworked side of each CH st until 1 st before marked corner. Work 3 SC TOG over next 3 sts. Work 1 SC into each st until 1 st before marked corner. Work 3 SC TOG over next 3 sts. Work 1 SC into each CH st to finish rnd, sl st to first SC of rnd. CH 1.

3 Handle round 2: Place markers at inside corners of handles. *Work 1 SC into each SC from prev rnd until 1 st before marked corner. Work 3 SC TOG over next 3 sts. Work 1 SC into each SC from prev rnd until 1 st before marked corner. Work 3 SC TOG over next 3 sts. Work 1 SC into each SC from prev rnd to finish rnd. Sl st into first SC of rnd. Change to yarn A and CH 1.

4 Handle rounds 3 and 4: Rep handle rnd 2.

5 Fasten off and weave in ends.

6 Follow directions for fulling in Chapter 11.

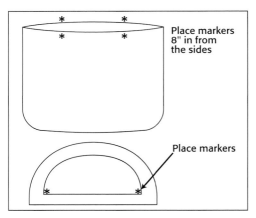

Place markers 8" in from the sides

Place markers

Spider Woman

Spin your own web and wear it to show off your skills! This pattern takes what you already know about working in the round and making arches and turns it all into a web motif.

MATERIALS

1 hank LanaKnits *All Hemp 6* (100% hemp, 150 yards/90g) in Sprout

5 mm hook

TECHNIQUES USED

CH Chain

SC Single crochet

DC Double crochet

TR Treble crochet

Working in the round

Mesh arches

Note: *See Chapters 3, 4, 5, and 9 for information about these techniques.*

FINISHED SIZE

45½ inches plus 12 inch tassles

GAUGE

4 arches (3 CHs and 1 SC) and 10 rows = 4 inches (10 cm)

CONTINUED ON NEXT PAGE

Spider Woman
(continued)

Make the Spider Woman

MAKE THE SPIDER WEB MOTIF

Use markers to help you keep your place as you follow this atypical pattern.

1 Start with an adjustable ring.

2 Round 1: CH 4; this CH counts as 1 DC and 1 CH. Work *1 DC, CH 1 into the ring. Rep from * 6 times and sl st into top of 3rd CH to join (8 DC total).

3 Round 2: CH 6, work 1 DC into first DC from prev rnd. CH 3, *DC into next DC from prev rnd, CH 3, Rep from * 5 times. SS over CH from beg of rnd.

4 Round 3: CH 8 (place markers in third and sixth CHs), work 1 DC into next DC from prev rnd, CH 6, DC into next DC from prev rnd, *CH 5, DC into next DC from prev rnd. Rep from * 6 times.

5 Work 4 SS, 1 in each CH from marker to marker. Remove markers.

6 CH 6 (place marker in fourth CH), DC into next DC from prev rnd, CH 7, DC into next DC from prev rnd, CH 7 (place marker in fourth CH), TR into next DC from prev rnd, CH 6, TR into next DC from prev rnd, place marker in this st), CH 5, DC into next DC from prev rnd. This is the end of this round.

7 CH 6 and turn. Work 1 DTR into TR with marker and remove marker. CH 6. Work 1 DTR into next DC from prev rnd. CH 4. Work 1 DTR into CH with marker and then remove marker.

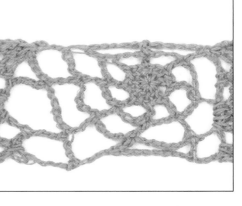

CREATE THE BODY

1 Row 1: CH 3, turn, SC in first CH space, CH 3, SC in next CH space, CH 3, SC in same CH space, CH 3, SC in same CH space, CH 3, SC in next CH space, CH 3, SC into DTR from prev row. CH 3, SC in same CH space, CH 3, and turn.

2 Row 2: Work 1 SC into first space created by chains from prev row. CH 3 and work 1 SC into next CH space. Rep from * until you have worked a SC into last CH space of row. CH 3 and turn.

3 Rep row 2 to desired length.

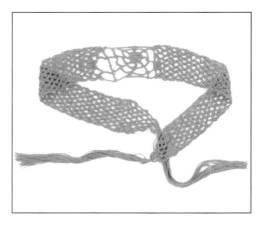

CROCHET THE TAPERED ENDS

1. Tapered row: Work 1 SC into first space created by CHs from prev row. CH 3 and work 1 SC into next CH space. Rep from * until last CH space; leave this space unworked. CH 3 and turn.

2. Rep tapered row until 1 arch is left.

3. Tie off and weave in ends.

4. Join yarn to other side of motif and work body pattern to same length.

5. Tie off and weave in ends.

MAKE THE TASSELS

With your arm bent at a 90-degree angle, tuck the yarn between your thumb and forefinger and wrap the yarn around your elbow many times. Cut the tassels and tie them to the tapered ends of the piece.

Magnificent Bamboo Scarf

Long double treble stitches make this graceful scarf work up quickly. Shells are worked in the middle of each row to create the increases that form a triangular shape, making this deceptively simple scarf magnificent.

Specifications

MATERIALS

1–3 skeins South West Trading Company *Bamboo* (100% bamboo, 135 yards/50g) in Tequila

5 mm hook

TECHNIQUES USED

CH   Chain

SC   Single crochet

DTR   Double treble crochet

Note: *See Chapters 3 and 5 for information about these techniques.*

FINISHED SIZE

One skein will make a scarf measuring 48 inches x 24 inches. For a larger scarf, add a second skein and keep working!

GAUGE

14 stitches and 4 rows = 4 inches (10 cm)

Make the Bamboo Scarf

1 CH 18.

2 Row 1: Work 1 SC into second CH from hook and into every CH across. CH 5 and turn.

3 Row 2: Work 1 DTR into first st and each of the next 7 sts. Into next st: [CH 1, 5 DTR, CH 1]. This shell creates the increases that shape the scarf. Work 1 DTR into each of the next 7 sts. Work 2 DTR into last st. CH 5 and turn.

4 Row 3: Work 1 DTR into each DTR from prev row. Work 1 DTR into CH 1 space and 1 DTR into each of the next 2 DTR from prev row. Into next st: [CH 1, 5 DTR, CH 1]. Work 1 DTR into each of the next 2 DTR from prev row and 1 DTR into CH 1 space. Work 1 DTR into each DTR from prev row until last st. Work 2 DTR into last st. CH 5 and turn.

5 Rep row 3 until scarf reaches the desired size.

6 Fasten off and weave in ends.

Cozy, Webby Sweater

This sweater is as cozy as it is contemporary. You use a large hook with two strands of DK-weight yarn to make a simple, webby fabric. The body is worked in one piece, reducing the amount of seaming necessary. You add the collar along the front and neck after the body is complete.

Specifications

See illustration on the next page for the schematic for this sweater.

MATERIALS

10 (10, 12, 12) balls South West Trading Company *Optimum DK* (154 yards/50g) in Silver

10 mm hook

TECHNIQUES USED

CH Chain

SC Single crochet

FLO Front loop only

Using increases and decreases for shaping

Note: *See Chapter 3 for information about these techniques.*

FINISHED SIZE

Bust/Chest circumference S (M, L, XL): 32–36 (38–42, 44–48, 50–54) inches

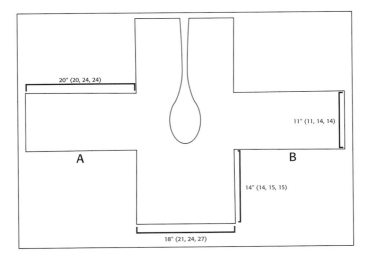

20" (20, 24, 24)

11" (11, 14, 14)

A

B

14" (14, 15, 15)

18" (21, 24, 27)

Make the Cozy, Webby Sweater

GET STARTED

You start this sweater at the bottom of the back and build out from there.

1 CH 38 (44, 52, 58).

2 Row 1: Work 1 SC into second CH from hook and each CH across. CH 1 and turn.

3 Row 2: Work 1 SC into FLO of each st in prev row. CH 1 and turn.

4 Repeat row 2 through row 28 (28, 30, 30)

INCREASE TO ADD SLEEVES

1 Row 29 (29, 31, 31): CH 39 (39, 45, 45).

This increase creates a sleeve on side A of the sweater.

2 Row 30 (30, 32, 32): Work 1 SC into second CH from hook and each CH across. Continue to work 1 SC into FLO of each st of prev row. CH 39 (39, 45, 45) and turn.

This increase creates a sleeve on side B of the sweater.

3 Row 31 (31, 33, 33): Work 1 SC into second CH from hook and each CH across. Continue to work 1 SC into FLO of each st of prev row. CH 1 and turn.

4 Row 32–35 (32–35, 34–39, 34–39): Work 1 SC into FLO of each st of prev row. CH 1 and turn.

5 At row 35 (35, 39, 39): Place a marker in the st, in the middle of the row.

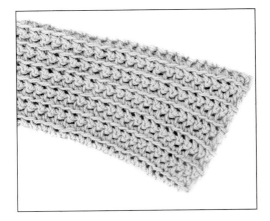

CONTINUED ON NEXT PAGE

WORK SIDE A

Row 36 (36, 40, 40): Work 1 SC into FLO of each st of prev row until you reach the marker. Work 1 SC into this st. CH 1 and turn.

SHAPE THE NECKLINE WITH DECREASES

1. Row 37 (37, 41, 41): Work 1 SC into FLO of first st and 2 SC TOG into FLO over next 2 sts. Continue across, working 1 SC into FLO of each st of prev row. CH 1 and turn.

2. Row 38 (38, 42, 42): Work 1 SC into FLO of each st of prev row. CH 1 and turn.

3. Row 39 (39, 43, 43): Work 1 SC into FLO of first st and 2 SC TOG into FLO over next 2 sts. Continue across, working 1 SC into FLO of each st of prev row. CH 1 and turn.

4. Row 40 (40, 44, 44): Work 1 SC into FLO of each st of prev row. CH 1 and turn.

5. *For small and medium sizes:*

   Row 41: Work 1 SC into FLO of each st of prev row. CH 1 and turn.

   For large and extra-large sizes:

   Row 45: Work 1 SC into FLO of first st and 2 SC TOG into FLO over next 2 sts. Continue across, working 1 SC into FLO of each st of prev row. CH 1 and turn.

6. Rows 42–48 (42–48, 46–50, 46–50): Work 1 SC into FLO of each st of prev row. CH 1 and turn.

SHAPE THE NECKLINE WITH INCREASES

1. Row 49 (49, 51, 51): Work 1 SC into FLO of first st and 2 SC into FLO of second st. Continue across, working 1 SC into FLO of each st of prev row. CH 1 and turn.

2. Row 50 (50, 52, 52): Work 1 SC into FLO of each st of prev row. CH 1 and turn.

3. Row 51 (51, 53, 53): Work 1 SC into FLO of first st and 2 SC into FLO of second st. Continue across, working 1 SC into FLO of each st of prev row. CH 1 and turn.

4 Row 52 (52, 54, 54): Work 1 SC into FLO of each st of prev row. CH 1 and turn.

5 Row 53 (53, 55, 55): Work 1 SC into FLO of first st and 2 SC into FLO of second st. Continue across, working 1 SC into FLO of each st of prev row. CH 1 and turn.

6 Row 54 (54, 56, 56): Work 1 SC into FLO of each st of prev row. CH 1 and turn.

7 *For small and medium sizes:*

Place marker at 39th st in from end of sleeve.

Row 55: Work 1 SC into FLO of first st and 2 SC into FLO of second st. Continue across, working 1 SC into FLO of each st of prev row until marked st. Work 1 SC into this st. CH 1 and turn.

Rows 56–84: Work 1 SC into FLO of each st of prev row. CH 1 and turn.

For large and extra-large sizes:

Row 57: Work 1 SC into FLO of first st and 2 SC into FLO of second st. Continue across, working 1 SC into FLO of each st of prev row. CH 1 and turn.

Row 58: Work 1 SC into FLO of each st of prev row. CH 1 and turn.

Place marker at 44th st in from end of sleeve.

Row 59: Work 1 SC into FLO of first st and 2 SC into FLO of second st. Continue across, working 1 SC into FLO of each st of prev row until marked st. Work 1 SC into this st. CH 1 and turn.

Rows 60–90: Work 1 SC into FLO of each st of prev row. CH 1 and turn.

WORK SIDE B

1 Row 36 (36, 40, 40): Join yarn at marked st and work 1 SC into this st. Work 1 SC into FLO of each st of prev row. CH 1 and turn.

2 Row 37 (37, 41, 41): Work 1 SC into FLO of each st of prev row. CH 1 and turn.

CONTINUED ON NEXT PAGE

SHAPE THE NECKLINE WITH DECREASES

1. **Row 38 (38, 42, 42):** Work 1 SC into FLO of first st and 2 SC TOG into FLO over next 2 sts. Continue across, working 1 SC into FLO of each st of prev row. CH 1 and turn.

2. **Row 39 (39, 43, 43):** Work 1 SC into FLO of each st of prev row. CH 1 and turn.

3. **Row 40 (40, 44, 44):** Work 1 SC into FLO of first st and 2 SC TOG into FLO over next 2 sts. Continue across, working 1 SC into FLO of each st of prev row. CH 1 and turn.

4. **Row 41 (41, 43, 43):** Work 1 SC into FLO of each st of prev row. CH 1 and turn.

5. *For small and medium sizes:*

   Row 42: Work 1 SC into FLO of each st of prev row. CH 1 and turn.

   For large and extra-large sizes:

   Row 44: Work 1 SC into FLO of first st and 2 SC TOG into FLO over next 2 sts. Continue across, working 1 SC into FLO of each st of prev row. CH 1 and turn.

6. **Rows 43–47 (43–47, 45–49, 45–49):** Work 1 SC into FLO of each st of prev row. CH 1 and turn.

SHAPE THE NECKLINE WITH INCREASES

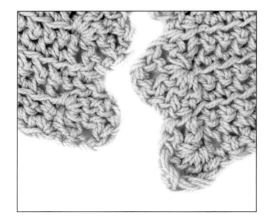

1. **Row 48 (48, 50, 50):** Work 1 SC into FLO of first st and 2 SC into FLO of second st. Continue across, working 1 SC into FLO of each st of prev row. CH 1 and turn.

2. **Row 49 (49, 51, 51):** Work 1 SC into FLO of each st of prev row. CH 1 and turn.

3. **Row 50 (50, 52, 52):** Work 1 SC into FLO of first st and 2 SC into FLO of second st. Continue across, working 1 SC into FLO of each st of prev row. CH 1 and turn.

4. **Row 51 (51, 53, 53):** Work 1 SC into FLO of each st of prev row. CH 1 and turn.

5. **Row 52 (52, 54, 54):** Work 1 SC into FLO of the first st and 2 SC into FLO of second st. Continue across, working 1 SC into FLO of each st of prev row. CH 1 and turn.

6. **Row 53 (53, 55, 55):** Work 1 SC into FLO of each st of prev row. CH 1 and turn.

For small and medium sizes:

Place marker at 39th st in from end of sleeve.

Row 54: Work 1 SC into FLO of first st and 2 SC into FLO of second st. Continue across, working 1 SC into FLO of each st of prev row until marked st. Work 1 SC into this st. CH 1 and turn.

Rows 55–84: Work 1 SC into FLO of each st of prev row. CH 1 and turn.

For large and extra-large sizes:

Row 57: Work 1 SC into FLO of first st and 2 SC into FLO of second st. Continue across, working 1 SC into FLO of each st of prev row. CH 1 and turn.

Row 58: Work 1 SC into FLO of each st of prev row. CH 1 and turn.

Place marker at 44th st in from end of sleeve.

Row 59: Work 1 SC into FLO of first st and 2 SCs into FLO of second st. Continue across, working 1 SC into FLO of each st of prev row until marked st. Work 1 SC into this st. CH 1 and turn.

Rows 60–90: Work 1 SC into FLO of each st of prev row. CH 1 and turn.

8 Fasten off and weave in ends.

FINISH THE SWEATER

1 Fold the sweater as shown in the illustration.

2 Use backstitch to seam from edge of sleeve across and down side of sweater.

3 Repeat to seam the other side of the sweater.

CONTINUED ON NEXT PAGE

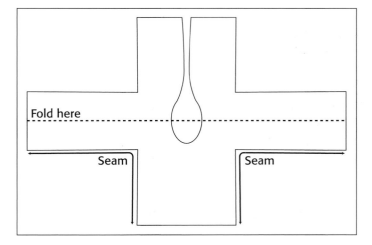

Fold here

Seam   Seam

CREATE THE COLLAR

1 Along the front and neck, you work this shell pattern into the sides of the rows in the body of the sweater:

2 Join yarn into row space at front bottom edge. *Work [1 DC, CH 1, 1 TR, CH 1, 1 TR, CH 1 and 1 DC] into space. Skip 1 row space and work 1 SC into next row space. Skip 1 row space. Rep from * along front sides and neck of sweater.

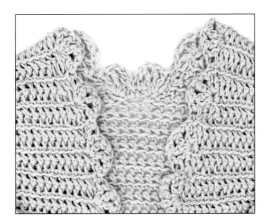

Rows with different stitch patterns and stripes of color create layers of yummy, cuddly stitches perfect for a blanket as stylish as it is scrumptious. Here you'll find everything you need to know to customize the pattern to the size you want.

Specifications

MATERIALS

Blue Sky Alpacas *Organic Cotton* (100% organic cotton, 150 yards/100g) in Shell (yarn A)

Blue Sky Alpacas *Dyed Cotton* (100% organic cotton, 150 yards/100g) in Nut (yarn B)

The amount of yarn you need depends on the size you choose to make:

> Baby Blanket: 9 skeins
> Bigger Blanket: 23 skeins

6 mm hook

TECHNIQUES USED

CH   Chain

SC   Single crochet

EHDC   Extended half double crochet

EHDC trinity cluster: Work 3 EHDC TOG into the same space as the last stitch and over the next 2 spaces

Note: See Chapters 3, 5, and 8 for information about these techniques.

CONTINUED ON NEXT PAGE

FINISHED SIZE

Baby Blanket: 40 inches x 44 inches

Bigger Blanket: 60 inches x 77 inches

Note: See "Gauge" for instructions on customizing your blanket if you'd like to make a different size.

GAUGE

10 stitches = 4 inches

10 rows = 5½ inches

This means that:

> Each repeat of 10 stitches adds 4 inches to the width.
> Each repeat of the 10-row pattern adds 5½ inches to the length.

Baby Blanket: 40 inches x 44 inches

> 4 inches x 10 repeats (100 sts) = 40 inches
> 5½ inches x 8 row repeats (80 rows) = 44 inches

Bigger Blanket: 60 inches x 77 inches

> 4 inches x 15 repeats (150 sts) = 60 inches
> 5½ inches x 14 row repeats (140 rows) = 77 inches

Make the Yummy, Scrumptious Blanket

WORK THE PATTERN

The foundation CH is equal to the number of sts required for the width plus 2 for the turning CH.

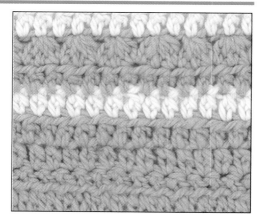

1 Baby Blanket: CH 102.

Bigger Blanket: CH 152.

2 Row 1: Work 1 EHDC into third CH from hook and into each CH across. CH 2 and turn.

3 Row 2: Work 1 EHDC into first EHDC from prev row. Work 1 EHDC trinity cluster starting in same st as prev EHDC and then into next 2 sts. *CH 1. Work 1 EHDC trinity cluster into same space as last st of prev cluster, and then into next 2 sts. Rep from * across row. Work 1 EHDC into same space as last st of prev trinity cluster.

4 Rows 3–5: Work 1 EHDC into first EHDC from prev row and into each st across. CH 2 and turn.

5 Row 6: Work 1 EHDC into first EHDC from prev row. *Work 2 EHDC into next EHDC from prev row. Rep from * across row until last st. Work 1 EHDC into last st. CH 1 and turn.

Note: Row 6 increases the number of sts in the row to create a change in texture. Row 7 decreases the number of sts back to the same number in each row prior to row 6.

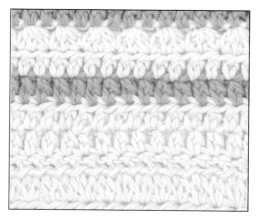

6 Row 7: Work 1 SC into first EHDC from prev row. *Skip next st and work 1 SC into following st. Rep from * across row. Work 1 SC into last st, CH 1, and turn.

7 Rows 8 and 9: Work 1 EHDC into first EHDC from prev row and each st across. Change to yarn B at end of row 9, CH 2, and turn. (See Chapter 4 for more on changing colors.)

8 Row 10: Work 1 EHDC into first EHDC from prev row and each st across. Change to yarn A at end of row, CH 2, and turn.

9 Row 11: Work 1 EHDC into first EHDC from prev row and each st across. CH 2 and turn.

10 Row 12: Rep row 2. Change to yarn B at the end of the row.

11 Row 13: Rep row 3.

12 Row 14: Rep row 4.

13 Row 15: Rep row 5.

14 Row 16: Rep row 6.

15 Row 17: Rep row 7.

16 Row 18: Rep row 8.

17 Row 19: Rep row 9. Change to yarn A at end of row.

18 Row 20: Rep row 10. Change to yarn B at end of row.

19 Row 21: Rep row 11.

20 Row 22: Rep row 2. Change to yarn A at end of row.

21 Row 23: Rep row 3.

22 Row 24: Rep row 4.

23 Row 25: Rep row 5.

24 Row 26: Rep row 6.

25 Row 27: Rep row 7.

26 Row 28: Rep row 8.

27 Row 29: Rep row 9. Change to yarn B at end of row.

28 Row 30: Rep row 10. Change to yarn A at end of row.

29 Rows 31–44 (Baby Blanket): Continue to work through repeating rows 11–24.

Rows 31–140 (Bigger Blanket): Continue to work through repeating rows 11–30.

30 Fasten off and weave in ends.

Index

Read Less–Learn More®

Visual®

Teach Yourself VISUALLY™ books...

Whether you want to knit, sew, or crochet...strum a guitar or play the piano...train a dog or create a scrapbook...make the most of Windows XP or touch up your Photoshop CS2 skills, Teach Yourself VISUALLY books get you into action instead of bogging you down in lengthy instructions. All Teach Yourself VISUALLY books are written by experts on the subject and feature:

- Hundreds of color photos or screenshots that demonstrate each step or skill

- Step-by-step instructions accompanying each photo
- FAQs that answer common questions and suggest solutions to common problems
- Information about each skill clearly presented on a two- or four-page spread so you can learn by seeing and doing
- A design that makes it easy to review a particular topic

Look for Teach Yourself VISUALLY books to help you learn a variety of skills—all with the proven visual learning approaches you enjoyed in this book.

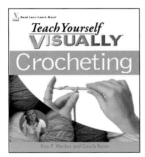

0-7645-9641-1

Teach Yourself VISUALLY™ Crocheting

Picture yourself crocheting accessories, garments, and great home décor items. It's a relaxing hobby, and this is the relaxing way to learn! This Visual guide *shows* you the basics, beginning with the tools and materials needed and the basic stitches, then progresses through following patterns, creating motifs and fun shapes, and finishing details. A variety of patterns gets you started, and more advanced patterns get you hooked!

0-7645-9640-3

Teach Yourself VISUALLY™ Knitting

Get yourself some yarn and needles and get clicking! This Visual guide *shows* you the basics of knitting—photo by photo and stitch by stitch. You begin with the basic knit and purl patterns and advance to bobbles, knots, cables, openwork, and finishing techniques—knitting as you go. With fun, innovative patterns from top designer Sharon Turner, you'll be creating masterpieces in no time!

0-7645-9642-X

Teach Yourself VISUALLY™ Guitar

Pick up this book and a guitar and start strumming! *Teach Yourself VISUALLY Guitar* shows you the basics photo by photo and note by note. You begin with essential chords and techniques and progress through suspensions, bass runs, hammer-ons, and barre chords. As you learn to read chord charts, tablature, and lead sheets, you can play any number of songs, from rock to folk to country. The chord chart and scale appendices are ready references for use long after you master the basics.

designed for visual learners like you!

0-7645-7927-4

0-7645-8840-0

Teach Yourself VISUALLY™ Windows® XP, 2nd Edition

...re than 150 Windows XP tasks. Learn how to ...count, load images from a digital camera, copy ...ore.

...toshop® CS2

...re than 150 Photoshop CS2 tasks. Learn how to ..., browse and sort images in Bridge, change image ...ne images, apply layer and filter effects, and more.

Available wherever books are sold.

Visual®
An Imprint of ⊕WILEY
Now you know.

Wiley, the Wiley logo, the Visual logo, Read Less-Learn More, and Teach Yourself Visually are trademarks or registered trademarks of John Wiley & Sons, Inc. and/or its affiliates.
All other trademarks are the property of their respective owners.